What
Happens
in Greece

BOOKS BY SUE ROBERTS

Greece Actually

Going Greek

Some Like It Greek

As Greek as It Gets

A Very French Affair

You, Me and Italy

My Very Italian Holiday

My Big Greek Summer

SUE ROBERTS

What Happens in Greece

Bookouture

Published by Bookouture in 2022

An imprint of Storyfire Ltd.
Carmelite House
50 Victoria Embankment
London EC4Y 0DZ

www.bookouture.com

ISBN: 978-1-80314-184-8
eBook ISBN: 978-1-80314-183-1

For Sophie, William and Lucy

PROLOGUE

I grab my water bottle and step outside into the blazing sunshine to enjoy a break from the house renovations, the old T-shirt and shorts I'm wearing covered in a light film of dust.

Taking in the long garden, I can't believe how beautiful it looks now, compared to the jungle it resembled three months ago when we first arrived here in Crete. My fiancé, Jamie, and our kind neighbour, Stelios, have worked so hard creating a wonderful, relaxing space, planting wildflowers and herbs along the borders in the shadow of a huge lemon tree.

I walk around the garden, inhaling the fragrance of rosemary and oregano. Further along, I brush past a lavender bush, releasing its heady scent.

Glancing at the olive grove beyond the white picket fence, I almost have to pinch myself. Does all this really belong to Jamie and me? As I watch our builder putting the finishing touches to the once dilapidated annexe that we soon hope to rent out, I feel a real sense of pride.

Jamie appears from the kitchen carrying a tray with bottled beers and two glasses, as I take a seat on the white, wrought-iron patio set on the covered terrace, alongside two comfy sunloungers.

'I think we've earned this.' He smiles, brushing plaster dust from his hair.

'I agree,' I say, abandoning my water and sipping the ice-cold beer.

As the sun beams down from a brilliant-blue sky, I thank my lucky stars for my life. I can't wait to see what the future holds for our new start in Greece. Everything I have ever wanted is right here in front of me.

1

I turn the vintage sign on the red front door to closed, just as an elderly gent called Eric, a regular at my café, appears outside, his mouth turned down in a look of disappointment. I quickly open the front door and usher him inside.

'Thanks, Charlie, you're a good'un. My wife would never have forgiven me if I'd gone home without her caramel latte.'

'Well, we can't have that now, can we, Eric?' I say.

'I didn't realise the time,' he explains, removing his grey cap as he steps inside. 'I got chatting to a bloke down by the river about his boat, and the time just flew by. I glanced at my watch and couldn't believe it was after six.'

I take some milk from the fridge and set the coffee machine to work. It's all shiny and clean, as I was about to switch it off for the evening. It's six twenty-five and the café is meant to close at six, but I never have the heart to turn customers away. I'd only just closed up after listening to another regular sound off about her teenage son, almost putting me off having kids for life.

'There you go then.' I hand Eric his wife's caramel latte and the 'normal' coffee for himself.

'Here, take these too. They'll only go in the bin otherwise.' I slide two Chelsea buns into a brown paper bag.

'Ooh, lovely. They're my wife's favourite! These will go down a treat when we watch *Emmerdale*. We generally don't have much at teatime, as we have a big lunch,' he informs me with a smile. 'Thanks again, love. See you soon.'

He leaves the shop beaming, and I'm so happy I invited him inside and gifted him the cakes. It's the small acts of kindness that make you feel good.

I love working in my little café near the banks of the River Dee in Chester and feel blessed to have such a lovely, varied clientele walk through my door every day. There are benches along the river where people often sit and watch the world go by, or the more active types canoe or take trips on riverboats. Chester is a great place to live and, despite the British weather, people regularly queue up for the boat trips in front of the café, often wearing cagoules and carrying umbrellas, determined to make the most of their leisure time.

I lock the door and head home, to the two-bedroomed apartment I bought with the money my lovely grandmother left me, and now share with Jamie. There's a tiny balcony at the flat, but what we'd really like is a house with a bit of a garden, so we're currently spending every spare second scouring estate agents' websites for something we might be able to afford together. But it would appear properties are being snapped up pretty quickly around here, and the ones that do come up in the location we want are way out of our price range.

I'm content living in Chester, I really am. But every now and then, I find myself thinking back to our recent holiday to Crete and wishing I was back there. I guess everyone feels like that after a holiday, but heading there always feels like going home. If I close my eyes, I can recall the heat on my skin and almost taste the delicious food. The smells of the almond trees, the cool sea breezes ruffling my hair as I walk along the beach.

Just lately, I've felt like every day here is the same. Work, home, weekends dining in the city centre with friends, babysitting for my nephew. I have a nice life and I don't want to appear ungrateful, but the truth is I'm craving a complete change. I've been feeling like this for months. I've been to Crete half a dozen times now and every time I step off the plane the pull is so strong that I feel like I've come home. Is it simply a fantasy to think that one day I might actually live there? Maybe so. But it never did anyone any harm to hold on to their dreams, did it?

2

I push the key in the door, and the first thing I do is release my hair from its high ponytail, dropping the band on the light oak table in the hall and letting my long, curly blonde hair bounce free.

I make myself a brew, then head into our neat lounge and fire up my laptop to see if any new properties have come onto the market today, but there aren't any. Nearly all of the recent ones are either unsuitable or under offer, so soon enough my cursor hovers over the 'property abroad' section. I click on 'properties for sale in Crete', where a new addition springs up before my eyes. It's a two-bedroomed house in Chania that needs a bit of TLC, but looks sound enough. It even comes with an olive grove and a generous piece of land. Viewing these properties is just a little daydream I have, something to fantasise about but which I always keep to myself. But then my eyes clock the price and I'm staggered. It's an absolute bargain! Scrolling through the interior photos, I see lots of old-fashioned-looking rooms, but it's definitely a good house. Okay, the garden is like a jungle and there's an outbuilding with broken windows and grass growing through cracks in the floor, but it has so much potential. And the outbuilding is a bonus – it could be turned into a living space, maybe even rented out. I realise I'm getting a bit carried away but I'm still lost in my daydream when I hear the sound of Jamie's key in the front door.

'Hi, babe, did you have a good day?' He plants a kiss on my cheek.

'I did thanks. Busy. I'm exhausted. How about you?'

I look into the lovely dark-brown eyes of my fiancé. He has matching dark-brown hair and a neatly trimmed beard. Every day I can't help but think how handsome he is. Jamie's one of those popular blokes who gets on equally well with men and women – everybody loves him. He could probably have his pick of the local ladies. Then again, he once told me I could have had my pick of anyone too, and 'had I never noticed how blokes stared when I walked into a room' – which I highly doubt, by the way – so I guess we are lucky to have found each other.

'Oh, you know, alright,' he continues as I follow him into the kitchen. 'That new boss of ours is a right tit, though.' He sighs. 'He's winding everybody up.' Jamie opens the fridge and glugs some orange juice down straight from the carton.

'Including you?'

'A bit. He's got no sense of humour, not like Jack did.' Nobody had a bad word to say about his old boss, Jack, who had recently retired. 'And he's a right jobsworth. Those lads work hard, they're always up against it – the customers want their cars fixed yesterday. Jack would turn a blind eye to the odd smoke break here and there, or nipping to the corner shop, as long as the work was all done. Everything's on the clock with Nick the knob. He's changed the whole atmosphere of the place.' He sighs again.

Jamie is a mechanic who works for a large, busy garage just outside the city centre.

'Never mind. Maybe he's just trying to establish himself. He might ease off a bit over time.'

'I hope so,' he grumbles.

It's Tuesday evening, which means it's Jamie's five-a-side football night, so he nips upstairs to get his kit ready and I settle myself back at my laptop.

'Go and relax for a bit now. Vent some of your frustration on the football pitch.' I say, when he's back downstairs.

'I will.' He drops a kiss on the top of my head.

'I see you've been browsing houses again, anything new on the market? he asks, nodding at the computer screen, that's displaying the familiar green logo of the estate agent.

'No, there's nothing new been added today.' I don't tell him I've been browsing properties in Crete. He'll think I'm not taking the house search here in Chester seriously.

'Have you seen a blue footy sock anywhere?' Jamie asks, as he stuffs his football kit into a sports bag. 'I only appear to have one.'

'Try the tumble dryer. I'm pretty sure they went in there as a pair.'

He goes off in search of his sock, and comes back waving it triumphantly.

'Nice one. Right, what do you fancy for dinner? I'll bring a takeaway home. Do you want Chinese or Indian?'

We always eat late on Tuesdays, as Jamie has football, so I try to have a late lunch too.

'Umm, Indian?'

'I'm glad you said that. I am just in the mood for a lamb bhuna.' He grins. 'See you later.'

I take a quick shower, then sit down on the sofa in my grey velour hoodie and pants. Our lounge has a modern style to it, made cosy with candles, colourful cushions and soft throws. I put a girlie movie on Netflix and settle down for the evening. I have a list of films that I'm working my way through when Jamie goes out to football, as he doesn't really enjoy romcoms. I pour myself a glass of white wine and watch as a cute story unfolds about a couple who are getting married in Rome, when a local lothario called Raphael catches the eye of the bride-to-be, making her doubt everything. It's just getting interesting when my phone rings. It's my older sister, Milly.

'Hey, hun, how's things?' I pause the movie.

'Good, thanks. Are you okay?'

'Fine. Pooped, but that's normal.' I take a slurp of wine.

'I was wondering, Charlie, if you're not busy that is...' She hesitates for a second. 'Could you do me a huge favour?'

I know what she's about to ask before the words even leave her lips.

'Go on.'

'Would you mind having Noah for a few hours? I'm going for a meal with a bloke called Sam. I'll collect him later tonight.'

Noah is my adorable six-year-old nephew. Milly is a year out of her relationship with Noah's dad, the bloke she thought she would be with forever. Her ex, Dan, obviously never shared this notion as he ran off with the yoga instructor from the classes he'd been attending to sort out his back problem. I pause, making her wait, although I'm sure she knows what my answer will be.

'Alright then. Drop him off whenever you're ready.' I imagine her punching the air.

'I owe you one. This bloke sounds amazing! He's a fireman.'

'Wait. Fireman Sam, really?'

'Gosh, I never even made the connection! Fireman Sam, yes!' She breaks into a fit of laughter.

'Who are you seeing next week? Bob the builder?' I tease.

Milly has recently discovered Tinder, and it seems there's no stopping her. She's been on three dates in the past fortnight, and even though the last two have been disastrous she seems determined to press on. The first turned out to be married – she had her suspicions and followed him home after one of their dates, where he was greeted by his wife with a kiss at the front door – and the second talked non-stop about his passion for fishing. He even chose fish for his starter and main course: the man was obsessed.

'There might not be a next time, if Sam turns out to be the one,' Milly says a little dreamily.

'Let's hope he isn't like your last date, with a hobby that he likes to talk about all evening.'

'Oh, don't remind me.' She laughs. 'There was no *plaice* in my life for someone like that.'

Half an hour later, fair-haired Noah has bounded into the flat and jumped onto the end of the large corner sofa. He's wearing a Chester football kit, a gift from Jamie on his last birthday.

'Can I watch *Ninja Turtles*, Auntie Charlie?' he asks hopefully.

It's hard to deny him anything when he looks at me with his large brown eyes, even though it's past his bedtime.

'Go on then. Would you like some popcorn?' I'm already standing up and heading for the kitchen.

'Yes, please.'

I return to the lounge with a bowl of popcorn and some apple juice before I search Netflix for the turtles movie, resigning myself to the fact that the delectable Raphael in my movie is being replaced by his namesake, albeit a big green reptile that likes to hang around sewers.

Later, Noah is yawning as the credits roll on the movie and Jamie returns home carrying a takeaway.

'Hiya, buddy, how are you?' He ruffles Noah's hair. 'I didn't know you were staying.' Jamie glances at me.

'Neither did I. Milly has a date,' I reply cheerfully.

'And I didn't know the turtles were a thing again. I used to watch this when I was a kid,' Jamie tells Noah as he sets out the curry at the dining table. He offers Noah some, but my nephew turns his nose up.

'Who's your favourite turtle? Mine was Leonardo. He was so cool.'

'I like Splinter. He teaches the turtles all their karate moves.' Noah stands up and Jamie laughs as he demonstrates one, almost falling over.

Milly told me she would collect Noah 'later', but it's now well past his bedtime, so I send her a quick text to ask how her date is going and to say that Noah can stay here overnight if she wants. It's the Easter holidays after all and Noah loves having a sleepover here.

She texts back to say the date is going well, thanking me and adding a kiss and heart emoji. I tell her I'll take Noah into the café with me tomorrow, and she can collect him after work. She replies with a pair of red lips and a load of kisses.

I like having Noah to stay, but I can't imagine having a child of my own just yet. It's great doing the fun things with Noah – watching movies, having days out and all of that stuff – but it's nice to go back to the retreat of the quiet flat after a busy day spent with him. Besides, having children is not really something that Jamie and I have discussed all that much, or at least not something we have made a decision about. Looking after Noah occasionally gives us the best of both worlds.

I nudge my nephew in the ribs gently. 'Right, come on. It's well past your bedtime, go and brush your teeth. You know where your pyjamas are. I'll be in to say goodnight shortly.'

Noah keeps a pair of pyjamas and a toothbrush here, which, thinking about it, is probably an open invitation for Milly. Not that I mind really, but I hope she wouldn't rely on me too much if the relationship got serious; my life is busy enough as it is.

When Noah is settled in bed and we've eaten the delicious curry, I bake a huge batch of brownies for tomorrow. I have a lady called Sue who makes scones and buns for me, as hers are far better than mine could ever be. She also helps out in the café during the lunchtime rush. Along with the cakes, tea and coffees, we also serve panini but nothing else. I did consider expanding the menu once, but decided that less is best, focusing on selling a few quality products. And judging by the lovely comments from my loyal customers, it would appear that they agree.

It's just after eleven o'clock when Jamie and I side into bed. He runs his hand along the inside of my thigh, but having Noah next door with paper-thin walls is a bit of a passion killer for me.

'You're too soft with that sister of yours,' says Jamie as he extends his arm for me to snuggle into.

'I know, but she's had such a hard time lately and she doesn't really have anyone else to ask. And it's nice to see her going on dates again.'

I really don't mind. Milly is such a wonderful mum to Noah. Since his dad's departure, she has spent every spare minute with Noah, taking him on lovely trips to zoos and parks, having his friends from school over for tea. It's only recently that she has tried the tricky task of fitting in dating too.

My parents left Chester two years ago and retired to a caravan park in Lancashire with views of the Ribble Valley. Although, in truth, I think even if they lived in Chester they would only occasionally offer to take Noah. I once heard Mum say – after she'd had a few glasses of wine – that she hadn't waited all these years for her retirement to be a babysitting service. The remark stung Milly at the time, who had probably thought that's exactly what our parents would be. Instead, she relies on after-school clubs, friends, and me and Jamie. And, of course, Noah does spend time with his father, Dan, who also offers some financial support. He takes him every other week-end, but with drop-offs and pick-ups, it doesn't leave Milly with that much time.

'I know that.' Jamie kisses me on my forehead. 'I'm just saying that you have a life, too. She can't expect you to be available for her at the drop of a hat.'

I know he's right, of course. And it makes my own daydream of living in Greece exactly that. A dream. I realise with clarity that lots of people need me here. Who would look after Noah if I were a plane ride away? A life in the sun will just have to remain on hold for now. I snuggle into Jamie, feeling the familiar touch of his skin against mine and, before I know it, I'm out like a light.

3

I wake early, make myself a coffee and put a batch of red velvet cupcakes in the oven before taking another peek at the newly available house in Crete on the website. I look at the clock and stifle a yawn – it's just after six. I work a long day at the café and I really ought to employ someone other than Sue, who's only with me for a couple of hours a day. The rest of the time I manage alone.

Jamie wakes up at seven and hops into the shower. When he's dressed, he strolls into the kitchen and drops some bread into the toaster, then sets about making a pot of coffee, passing a mug to me. Two minutes later, Noah pads into the kitchen, rubbing his eyes.

'Morning, sleepyhead. Do you fancy pancakes for breakfast?' I retrieve a jug of batter mix that I'd prepared along with the cupcakes from the fridge.

'Pancakes? Now you tell me.' Jamie pulls a face before taking a bite of his toast and glugging down his coffee.

'I'll make you some at the weekend,' I promise.

'I'll hold you to that. Right, got to go. Don't want that new boss on my case.' He high fives Noah. 'See you soon, buddy.'

Jamie whispers in my ear after kissing me goodbye and squeezing my hand. 'Maybe we'll have an early night? Make sure it's a child-free zone this evening.'

'I will do.' My heart rate quickens at the thought. Even though apathy may have set in when it comes to other parts of my daily routine, Jamie is the one thing guaranteed to still get my pulse racing.

After the front door closes and I've cooked a stack of pancakes to keep Noah busy, I quickly peer at my laptop and start to read about the house in more detail. It's in a little village, less than an hour's drive from Chania, with its bustling Venetian harbour filled with shops and restaurants. As I read through the listing again, I realise it has had a price reduction from its already bargain price, and can't help wondering why. I imagine it will get snapped up now. I sigh as I close my laptop and wonder if we will ever have a place with some outside space. There's been a real price hike in the area lately, and although that obviously includes our apartment, it still means the gap between our flat and our dream home is getting bigger. We've already missed out on several houses. Ten properties, to be exact, have been snapped up the second they appeared on the market, offered higher bids than we could ever afford. I'm honestly not sure I can face the heartache of missing out on yet another place, but I don't want to give up on my dream of one day having a house with a lovely garden, like the one I grew up in as a child that had an apple tree in the centre of the lawn.

I close my laptop and get ready for another day at work. As Noah and I are about to leave, I grab a hooded jacket from a coat hook, seeing dark clouds gathering in the sky.

Noah sits quietly colouring at a little table in front of the counter as I make a tuna panini and a takeaway coffee for a bloke in paint-splattered overalls.

The café is small, with just four tables inside and two outside for when the weather is fine. Most of the business is takeaway, although the outside tables are constantly occupied when the sun shines.

I nip out after the lunchtime rush before Sue leaves at two, and walk with Noah along the banks of the river. The dark clouds have thankfully blown over and the sun has finally broken through. Noah and I take a seat on a bench after we've bought ice creams: strawberry for me, and chocolate for Noah. We're watching a boat take tourists on a trip down the River Dee. Some of the boats here even offer afternoon tea cruises and party evenings.

'I like boats,' says Noah as he licks his ice cream. 'I've been on that big one.' He points to the red and white river cruiser. 'My dad took me out on a rowing boat too.'

My heart suddenly goes out to Noah.

'Have you got used to your dad not living at home?' I ask him gently.

He shrugs. 'A bit. He lives far away now but he's decorating a bedroom for me so I can have more sleepovers.'

'Where do you sleep now then?' I ask.

'In Daddy's room on a big sofa bed. The spare bedroom is full of stuff. I'm having Spider-Man wallpaper when he decorates it.'

'That sounds great!'

'And he lives near a science museum that he's going to take me to next time.' He turns his attention to his ice cream once more, and I sincerely hope things work out between him and his dad.

Just before two o'clock we're back at the café and Noah is counting money into little plastic bank bags when Milly walks through the door. I'm impressed with his counting and money skills, although Milly did tell me that Noah is on the top table for maths in his class.

'You're early.' I smile, happy to see her. She's brandishing a huge bunch of flowers that she hands to me.

'Thanks for having Noah, sis. I really do appreciate it.'

'Oh, wow, they're beautiful, thanks. And it's a pleasure having him, of course. Have you finished work early?'

Milly works at the local library and doesn't usually finish until around five.

'I was owed a couple of hours in lieu of a recent course I attended. Thought I'd take them today and take Noah to the cinema. If you fancy it?' she says, catching Noah's eye.

'Yeah!'

Noah has already abandoned his coin sorting and leapt off his chair to run and cuddle his mum. Milly always oozes elegance and today she's wearing a pale-blue dress, with a white scarf adorned with flowers casually draped around her neck. A cream cardigan thrown over the top completes the look. Her caramel highlights in her neat bob look expensive, although she has them done at a local hairdresser. Her clothes are often supermarket brands too, but she's one of those people who manage to carry everything off with style and elegance, always looking well groomed. I glance down at my red pinny with some of the stitching coming away, and the strands of my curly hair escaping my hairband. As I swoop it back up, I laugh at how different we are.

'Can we watch *Aquaman 2*?' Noah asks Milly hopefully, jumping up and down with excitement.

'Oh, go on then,' replies Milly, smiling at her son.

'You're all heart, you. Fancy having to endure two hours of Jason Momoa.' I raise an eyebrow and she laughs.

'I know, the sacrifices we make for our kids.' She places her hand on her heart. 'Thanks again for having him, sis. I'll see you soon.'

Noah is already halfway out of the door, asking if he can have popcorn and pick 'n' mix at the cinema, leaving just me and Sue in the café.

'I was wondering,' says Sue as she's tidying around, sweeping the floor and wiping a couple of tables before she leaves. 'Are you looking for any more help? Maybe at the weekends? You never seem to have any time off.'

It's true. But that's what it is like when you have your own business, I suppose. I like to make sure everything is just so, and I can only do that if I'm here. My good reputation has to continue, especially as I've noticed one or two other cafés popping up of late not far from here.

'Are you after more hours?' I ask, as I mull over her suggestion.

'No, I was thinking more of my niece, Pixie. She's seventeen and at college and is after a part-time job. She's a great kid, hard working.'

It does get busy at the weekends, and there's no doubt I'd like an hour here or there to nip out to the shops or something, although sometimes Jamie does pop down and serve behind the counter on Saturday afternoons and we head home together. I open at eleven on a Sunday, but the café is never closed for the whole day at any point in the week.

'Actually, that might not be a bad idea.'

I know Jamie would jump at the chance to be freed up on Saturday afternoons so he can watch the football. He supports our local team, Chester F.C., and occasionally makes the journey to Anfield with a couple of mates to watch Liverpool.

'If you could mention it to her, I'd be happy for her to come over and have a trial in the café,' I tell Sue.

'Really? That's brilliant, thanks, Charlie. I'm sure she'll jump at the chance.'

. . .

I lock up at six on the dot this evening and head home, calling in at a local Sainsbury's for some red wine, so I can have a glass with dinner.

Jamie and I arrive home almost at the same time and, after showering, we're both sitting in the kitchen as I rustle up an evening meal.

'Mmm, that smells amazing. I would have cooked, you know.' He stands behind me and snakes his arms around my waist, gently kissing my neck.

'Stop, you're putting me off!' I laugh as I almost tip a whole jar of dried chilli flakes into the mix.

'Oh, cheers.' He laughs, before opening the wine and pouring me a glass. He then grabs himself a bottle of beer from the fridge.

'You know what I mean. So how was your day?' I ask as I set a pan down to simmer on the stove.

Jamie lets out a deep sigh. 'Alright, I suppose. But I won't lie, that new boss is still making the place feel like a workhouse.' He sips his beer. 'I wish we were back in Crete. But I suppose everyone feels like that when they've had a great holiday. I just love it there.'

'I know, me too.'

It's where we got engaged after all, two years ago, so I guess it's always going to be a special place for us.

We're eating chilli, and I'm trying to resist a third piece of garlic bread, when the subject of house hunting comes up again. This time, I decide to tell Jamie about my sneaky searches of places in Greece.

'I'm not sure we could afford a holiday home, if we're also looking for a new house here,' he says. 'By the way, this food is amazing. I'm taking you out to dinner on Saturday to say thank you.'

I laugh, as we've already arranged a night out at a city centre restaurant with some friends Saturday evening.

When we've cleared away and we're sitting on the sofa relaxing, I gently bring our discussion back round to houses.

'I know it sounds like a wild idea, but why just a holiday home? Why couldn't we sell up and actually move there?'

There's silence for a moment as Jamie processes my words. 'Are you serious?' He stares at me as if I've suggested a trip to the moon.

'I dunno. Sorry, I know it's a mad idea, it's just that I saw this place on a website and it could be absolutely perfect. With a little sprucing up, that is. I can't stop thinking about it. I'm just dreaming, though, I realise that our life is here.'

'There's nothing wrong with having dreams. Let's have a look then.' He grabs the laptop from the coffee table and fires it up. Minutes later, we're staring at the whitewashed house with a dazzling blue sky in the background. The garden is a mass of thistles and wildflowers, and there's the outbuilding with its cracked windows and missing roof tiles. Even in that state though, there's no denying how beautiful it is. Jamie almost spits his beer out when he sees the price.

'Wow. We could sell this place and still have money in the bank.' He scrolls through the images. And even though the lounge only has a log-burning stove and although the interior is dated, Jamie agrees the potential of the place is undeniable.

'Not forgetting the sale of the café,' I remind him. 'That could fund the renovation. That outbuilding could be restored to become a holiday annexe. We'd have to earn a living out there, of course.'

'You'd sell the café?' Jamie looks shocked. 'But it's your life. You've built that up from nothing.'

I'd snapped up the premises, which had previously been a mobile phone store, and lovingly restored it to the cosy café that it is now. In fact, that's where we met, when Jamie called in one afternoon for a takeaway coffee and I hadn't secured the lid properly. It came spurting out as he lifted it, luckily only ending up on the floor, rather than over his rather fetching blue shirt. I was mortified, and he accepted my apologies on the proviso that I take him out to dinner the following evening. As it turned out, he was a perfect gentleman and paid the bill in full, laughing at me for thinking that he would actually expect me to foot the cost of dinner in the city over a spilled coffee. That was almost four years ago and the rest, as they say, is history.

'The café is my life, but maybe that's the point. It consumes my life. Don't get me wrong, I love what I do, but just lately, well, everything feels a bit samey. I feel as though I'm ready for a complete life change.'

Jamie's eyes are suddenly wide as he drums his fingers on the arm of the sofa. I know that restless look. It's the same look he gets when he's about to announce something fun and sponta-neous. Like the time I told him I'd always wanted to visit the Christmas markets in Prague. He booked the flights at five o'clock that very afternoon and we boarded the plane three hours later.

'We should book a viewing,' he says decisively.

'You're serious?' I can't tell if it's just the beer talking.

'Why not? No harm in having a look. Any excuse to go back to Crete. I've only got four days of annual leave left though until the end of June.'

'That's enough for a viewing trip. I don't want to leave the café for too long, anyway. But I'd have to speak to Sue first.' Sue is usually happy to cover my holidays since she's retired, as she told me she enjoys the contact with people, especially since her husband passed away. I don't want to exhaust her though as we only went away last month. Perhaps now is a good time to have Sue's niece work a few hours in the café. 'Are you serious about this, Jamie?' I ask, wondering if it's just a knee-jerk reaction to his rotten day at work with the new boss.

'Yep.' He nods his head slowly as he mulls it over. 'Why not?' He turns to me with a look of excitement on his face.' We should have a go at something different while we're still young enough to do it; we're only thirty-one after all. Maybe it's time for a bit of an adventure.' The enthusiasm in his voice is clear. 'And let's face it, there's not much chance of getting a house with a garden around here any time soon, is there? Moving abroad could be the solution. And we both have trades, so it's not that big a risk if things don't work out and we have to return, is it?'

He's right: people will always want bakers and mechanics.

I never thought Jamie would even consider such a notion, although I shouldn't get ahead of myself. It's only a viewing trip after all and, as Jamie said, any excuse to get back into the sunshine for a few days is worth a shot.

'Right, that's enough talk for one evening.' Jamie places my wine glass on the table, leans over and kisses me deeply. We sink back into the sofa together and I don't think I've ever felt as happy as I do right now.

4

'Hi, sis, how was the cinema?'

I give Milly a quick ring as I'm buying some hairspray and a new lipstick from Boots, ready for my night out this evening. I gave Pixie a trial on Friday, and she is as speedy and efficient as I was told she would be, so I've offered her a part-time job. I've left her alone for half an hour, as it's late in the afternoon and pretty quiet.

'Hi, Charlie. It was fun thanks. Noah loved it.'

We chat for a few minutes as I walk along, and she tells me how she caught someone in the library yesterday trying to steal a book by placing it at the bottom of her child's pram.

'I mean, who would steal a book from a library, for goodness' sake? You can borrow them for free!'

'I don't know. What book did she try to steal?'

She laughs. 'It was *Wuthering Heights*. Apparently, she'd been scouring second-hand shops for it. She'd read it at school and had a yearning to re-read it. It came as a revelation to her when I explained that she could keep renewing the book for as long as she liked, after she told me that she'd never have time to read it quickly, not with two young children. I ended up feeling a bit sorry for her. Oh and two cheeky schoolkids came in and asked did I have a copy of *The Edge of the Cliff* by Eileen Dover.'

'Better than asking for something by Ben Dover,' I reply and we both laugh.

'Actually, sis, while you're on the phone, I don't suppose you could do me a favour and babysit Noah this evening?' I can imagine my sister crossing her fingers and looking upwards in hope.

'I can't, Milly, I'm sorry. We're out with the gang in town this evening.' I feel a little bad for letting her down, but then I recall Jamie's words about not being so readily available. It is short notice for a Saturday evening, after all.

'Of course, sorry, it was selfish of me to ask on a Saturday night. It's just that Sam has invited me over to his place to cook dinner. I could take Noah, I suppose, but I'm not ready to introduce him just yet, not until I'm really sure he's going to be around for a while.'

I feel a pang of conscience. My sister is so careful to protect Noah's feelings – despite her occasional last-minute call for me to help out with babysitting. A sudden thought pops into my head.

'Why don't you hire a babysitter? That is, unless, you're planning to stay over,' I tease.

'I wasn't. I've only been out with him once. But even if I wanted to hire someone, I'm not sure who would be free on a Saturday evening.'

'Let me call you back in ten minutes.'

When I return to the café, I'm surprised to find a queue and Pixie looking ever so slightly flustered, although coping well.

'Gosh, Pixie, I'm sorry, it was so quiet when I left.' I quickly take an order from the next customer in the line.

'It's okay.' She smiles brightly as she prepares a cappuccino.

'Are you off out this evening?' I ask her ten minutes later, and she tells me no, she isn't and that she's trying to save some money for Creamfields music festival in August. 'I go out some weekends, but I never have enough money. I'm made up I've got this job.'

'Do you fancy earning a bit more this evening?' I tell her all about Noah.

'Of course, I'd love to!' She jumps at the chance. I call Milly, who was just about to head into town with Noah in tow. They call into the café and make arrangements. Noah bonds with Pixie instantly when she makes him a chocolate milkshake using some chocolate syrup that I keep in a cupboard, especially for Noah.

'She's great,' I whisper. 'She's Sue's niece, a student, so not some random stranger. She has two younger brothers so she's used to looking after boys. Maybe this could work out for you?'

'Oh, I hope so, thanks, Charlie. Not that I'm going to be out gallivanting every evening. I couldn't do that to Noah. I'll make sure Pixie gets a taxi home.' Milly beams.

I grab a tenner from my purse. 'Let me pay for that then. You pay the babysitting fee.'

Jamie would probably say I'm too soft, but it makes me happy to know that everyone else in my life is happy. And where's the harm in that?

5

We're heading for a trendy Italian restaurant in Lionsgate, a popular area of the city lined with restaurants and bars. There are remnants of the Roman occupation everywhere in Chester, with its old city walls and cobbled streets, as well as an amphitheatre that's being excavated. Shops and restaurants are nestled inside black-and-white, half-timbered buildings.

As we enter the cosy restaurant, it's pouring down outside and I place my umbrella in a bucket on the tiled floor by the entrance. There's also a traditional wooden coat stand, where I hang my white blazer that I threw on over a black jumpsuit.

Matty and Steph are already seated, along with Jade and Stuart, who we've only known for a year after meeting on holiday and discovering they lived locally. Steph has been my friend since high school and we've always been there for each other, especially after break-ups. She's been married to Matty for three years now after getting engaged following five years of dating. Luckily Matty and Jamie quickly became best friends, too, when we started dating a few years ago.

The six of us regularly meet up for evenings out. In good weather our friends will host BBQs but we can't yet return the favour as we only have our little terrace. Another reason we need to sell up and find somewhere with some outside space.

It's not long after we take a seat and order that our delicious bruschetta starters arrive, the enticing waft of garlic and herbs filling the air as our waiter sets the food down in front of us.

'Any joy with the house search?' asks Matty, as he sips a glass of Moretti beer.

Jamie and I exchange a glance.

'There's not a lot around here, to be honest. Houses seem to be getting snapped up really quickly at the moment,' says Jamie.

'I know. There's been a real price surge in the area too,' adds Steph. 'I worry things might be out of our reach if we want to move to a bigger house in the future, but I guess our place is increasing in value too.'

'I am not moving again,' Matty mutters to no one in particular and Steph pokes her tongue out at him playfully.

I tell them all about the Greek house on the website and how we are going to Crete to take a look at it. Steph's fork hovers in front of her open mouth.

'You're thinking of moving to Greece?'

'Possibly. It might be nothing more than a daydream, but there's no harm in having a look. You know how much we both love Greece.'

'For holidays, yes. I never thought you'd contemplate actually living there though. Gosh, I'd miss you.' Steph takes a bite of crusty bread covered with pesto. 'Our Saturday nights out just won't be the same without you guys.'

'No offence taken.' Jade laughs and Steph apologises for her gaffe.

'I'm not sure I could live abroad,' says Matty thoughtfully. 'I think I'm too much of a home bird.'

'Yeah, it must be hell living in the sun, sipping beer at the end of the day and watching the sun go down,' says Stuart, and the others laugh along with him.

I ask everyone about their week, not wanting our viewing trip to Greece to dominate the evening, and we laugh and drink and have a wonderful time. The food has been amazing, as usual, and the company even more delightful. We head to a bar with live music after our meal, and it's just after midnight when the others climb into a taxi. One thing we can't grumble about is the location of our apartment. It's in the city centre, which means we can walk home after an evening on the town.

Thankfully, the rain has stopped and I link my arm through Jamie's as we walk the streets, passing throngs of other people heading home after an evening out, or on to a nightclub, their loud chatter filling the air.

'I really enjoy our nights out with friends. I think that's one of the things I would miss,' Jamie tells me as we walk, our arms now around each other.

'Me too, but hopefully they would be regular visitors. And I'm sure we would make some new friends too. Anyway, I'm just keen to get back over there for a few days and sit in the sun.' I pull my blazer tightly around me as the evening air is quite chilly. I guess Jamie's right, we would miss our friends and I still have pangs of guilt over Milly and Noah. But still, we have to live the life we both desire.

'Are we taking those pancakes back to bed?' Jamie asks hopefully, the following morning, as he appears bleary-eyed in the kitchen and pours us both a coffee.

'I'm wide awake now,' I tell him as I pile the pancakes onto a plate and add a few blueberries. I've been awake since seven thirty, which is a lie-in for me.

'Who said anything about sleeping?' he says with a smile.

I'm waiting for a tray of brownies and a carrot cake traybake to come out of the oven. 'They'll be ready in five minutes.'

'You'll be back in time for them,' he says cheekily.

'You really know how to charm a girl.' I dip a teaspoon in the end of the batter mixture and flick it at him and it lands on the tip of his nose. He grabs a spoon and fires back, and a blob lands in my hair. As we're giggling, suddenly the oven timer goes off.

I take the brownies and carrot squares out of the oven to cool, laughing at Jamie, who still has a blob of batter in his hair.

'We're going to have to take a shower now,' says Jamie, taking me by the hand and leading me into our large bathroom with stone-coloured tiles, chrome fittings and large fluffy towels. I relish our Sunday mornings as I only open at noon, but I wish everything else wasn't on such a strict timetable: I want leisurely days in the sun. I can barely wait for our trip to Greece!

6

The following week, we step off the plane and inhale the scent of our favourite Greek island. Soon enough, we are heading off in a hire car and I wind the window down and feel the wind blowing through my hair, which will probably look like a burst mattress later, but I don't care. We head towards the village, a fifty-minute drive from Chania, with a feeling of excitement. The main street has a couple of restaurants and bars, a pharmacy and small general store on a tree-lined road that curves upwards to some houses. We pass a village square with a playground and a small general store nearby. Off the square is another bar, and a shop that has been closed down.

Parking up, close to the main street, we take a seat at an outside table of a café, under the shade of a tree and a young waiter quickly takes our order for coffees. A couple of locals at a nearby table look our way and say *kalimera* as they enjoy their lunch. I'm instantly reminded of how friendly the Greek people are, which is one of the reasons I long to live here. People are always in such a hurry back home, dashing about, complaining that there aren't enough hours in the day.

After our coffee stop, we drive in a loop, taking in the sights of the village until we're almost back near the tree-lined main street. I'm looking at the photo of the house on my phone, and for a short while we can't spot it as we walk along, although we know we are heading in the right direction. Suddenly, through a gap in some trees, we glimpse a FOR SALE sign and the house reveals itself in all its glory.

'Jamie, there it is!' I squeal excitedly as we head towards the house, discovering to our delight that the house is no more than a five-minute walk from the main street. As we approach the white house, which is bathed in bright sunlight, I can't help but feel a surge of excitement. And judging by the squeeze of my hand from Jamie and the huge smile on his face, I'm pretty sure he's feeling it too.

It's even more beautiful than in the photos online, a traditional Greek house surrounded by a large garden and olive trees in the background. A dark-haired estate agent wearing a floral dress greets us outside the house with a beaming smile.

'Your garden needs a little work, but it is large.' She waves her arm around the vast space, currently wild and unkempt. 'And, of course, you have the olive grove.' She gestures to an area behind a broken fence.

'What? That would belong to us?' Jamie asks in shock.

'Yes. This is one of the larger houses in the village, so it has more land.'

'I'm not sure I see myself as an olive farmer,' says Jamie with a laugh.

Inside, the lounge and kitchen need updating, but the agent tells us that the house is structurally sound, which hopefully the survey will bear out. The lounge has cute windows, with wooden shutters, that we hadn't really noticed before. And although the kitchen has several cracks in the floor tiles and a cupboard door is hanging off, it doesn't feel like it needs a major refurbishment. Climbing the creaky stairs, I scream and almost lose my footing when a bird flies through an open window on the landing. The window is made from beautiful stained glass, with a picture of a church, that I hadn't noticed online. Jamie manages to shoo the bird again, before closing the window firmly, and the pretty colours of the glass are reflected in a beautiful mirror that bathes the hall in a soft hue.

I smile as I enter the larger of the two bedrooms that is light and airy, with blue shutters at the window. There is also a metal fireplace, currently housing a large display of dried wildflowers. The estate agent tells us the house has stood empty for a while, hence the overgrown garden. I close my eyes and visualise a beautiful home, with white painted walls, homely soft furnishings and a modern kitchen and can hardly wait to get started.

When the estate agent leaves, with us promising to be in touch as soon as we've discussed things, we head down into the village street to a local restaurant called The Fig Tree, which we spotted on the drive in.

A tall man with stylish dark hair is chatting to a group of diners and greets us as we enter, showing us to a table. It's beneath the shade of a pergola with grape vines threaded through the roof, a welcome break from the heat. We order ice-cold beers and sip them as we order some food and wait for it to arrive.

'What do you think then?' I ask Jamie excitedly. 'Is it the one?'

My heart is beating wildly, hoping he has fallen in love with the house as much as I have.

'I think it is.' He smiles and I stamp my feet, and do a little happy dance in my chair.

'So do you think we should put an offer in?' I ask, holding my breath.

'One hundred per cent. There's no way we should lose that one. I think it's perfect for us.' He leans across the table and kisses me, and I feel like the happiest girl in the world.

After we've polished off our plates, the dark-haired man

approaches our table and asks if we would like anything else. He introduces himself as Darius, the owner of the restaurant. He's well groomed and looks somewhere in his mid-thirties.

'No, thank you, and that was delicious.' We have dined on the most delicious Greek salad and an assortment of creamy dips with pitta bread.

'You are here on holiday?' he asks and we explain that we have been looking at a house in the village.

'We're actually thinking of buying it,' Jamie reveals. 'In fact, we've decided we are going to put an offer in.'

'I know the house,' he tells us. 'It has stood empty for a little while after the owner sadly lost his wife and left the village. It will be nice for it to have some life breathed into it once more.' His face breaks into a smile.

'Thanks, we're looking forward to transforming it into our forever home.'

'Well, I hope you will be very happy here. It is a good place to live.' He smiles before heading off to greet a family who are looking at a menu board outside.

'Right, shall we get that offer in before someone else snaps it up?' Jamie takes his phone from his pocket.

'You're absolutely sure?' I ask.

'Positive. Let's do this. As long as you are too? Let's be honest, it's your money we are using.'

'Yes! I'm certain.' I almost scream with excitement as he puts in the call. Ten minutes later, our offer has been accepted.

'We've done it, I can hardly believe it. I can't believe we're doing this!' We lean in and hug each other, as I hold back tears of emotion.

'What do you think of the village?' I ask Jamie as we drive back to the hotel in Chania where we will be staying for a few days.

'I liked it. It had a really good feel about it. And I didn't realise it was so close to Platanias: there's plenty of bars and restaurants there.'

'I know, and a short drive to Chania and the airport too. It's perfect. Oh, Jamie, I can't believe we have actually bought a house here! It's like a dream come true.'

'I know, and I'm really looking forward to getting stuck in and transforming it. That outbuilding could be a really great place once it's done up. I don't think we'd ever be short of visitors,' says Jamie, his voice full of enthusiasm for the project.

'We'd need the outbuilding to rent out to paying guests, so we can earn a living,' I remind him.

'Suppose so.'

It's early evening when we arrive at the hotel and we stroll along the harbour of Chania. Even though it's only April, the evening is balmy and warm, the sky marbled with pink and lilac. The Venetian fortress looms in the skyline and boats bob in the harbour, one or two returning from day trips. We head into a bar for a snack and Jamie is delighted to find a football match being shown on a big screen.

'I wish we didn't have to go home in a couple of days,' Jamie says as he sips his beer and relaxes into the evening. 'I'm not exactly looking forward to going back to work.'

'Then don't think about it. Enjoy the time we have here.' I squeeze his hand.

We get chatting to a group of holidaymakers from Yorkshire who are surprised when we tell them we're over here on a viewing trip to buy a house.

'I wish I had the guts to do that,' says one of the blokes.

'Me too,' says a striking brunette with long eyelashes and perfectly shaped brows. 'I'm a beauty therapist so maybe I could open a salon somewhere.' She glances through the window at the throngs of holidaymakers walking through the streets, many of them immaculately groomed women.

'I don't think you'd be short of customers,' I comment.

'What will you do for work?' one of the blokes asks Jamie.

'I'm a mechanic, so I'm hoping to get a bit of work in a garage. Hopefully our main income will come from renting out the annexe though,' he tells him.

Jamie is going to hand his CV in to some garages in the area, but I'm worried there might be a language barrier, so I guess we will have to wait and see. Maybe it will give him the motivation he needs to try and master the language.

The men discuss the merits of the football match, deciding who needs a transfer and who had a lousy game, with all the authority of a Premiership manager.

Walking back to our hotel later, we pass the lighthouse at the end of the pier: a landmark familiar from our previous holidays here. A couple are walking along the pier towards it, holding hands as the sun begins to drop. On the harbour front, a jolly-looking busker wearing a red cap is playing an accordion and singing some Greek melody, as tourists throw coins into his tin. I find a couple of euros in the pocket of my long shorts to add to the collection and he nods in gratitude.

Passing the plethora of restaurants, their lights reflecting onto the water, Jamie and I stop for a cappuccino. As darkness falls, speedboats moor up for the evening alongside fishing boats that will head out as soon as dawn breaks to catch the fish for the restaurants.

Finishing our drinks, we take a short walk to the hotel, heading down a side street where the drone of a moped can be heard somewhere in the distance. We stroll past sand-coloured three-storey buildings with wrought-iron balconies and white houses with blue-painted front doors, before we arrive at our hotel, illuminated by a white sign beckoning us towards it, along with solar lights that are dotted along the path that leads up to the entrance.

As we head inside, I feel a warm, comfortable feeling in the pit of my stomach. I can imagine actually living here, spending lazy evenings watching the sun go down and taking strolls along the harbour. And peering at Jamie's smiling face as we walk, I'm pretty certain he feels the same.

7

We've been home for a few days now and everything is moving ahead full pelt. I woke even earlier than usual this morning, and decided to take a walk through the city before I head to the café. I walk over the cobbled streets, and near Bishopsgate I climb the stairs and walk along the city walls. I pass my favourite café on the walls, which is also a bookshop, and recall all the happy times I've spent browsing the shelves there on my rare days off from work, enjoying its quaint, quirky interior.

I descend the walls at another point, back into the shopping areas with the distinctive black-and-white buildings, rubbing shoulders with the red-bricked buildings that house modern and independent shops. A smartly dressed couple carrying expensive-looking suitcases are heading into the Chester Grosvenor Hotel, a rather grand hotel in the city centre. I once had a lovely afternoon tea there in its sumptuous dining room, decorated in rich golds, a chandelier hanging from the ceiling. If I'm honest though, even though it was faultless, I prefer things a little more rustic, which is probably why I'm such a fan of Greek tavernas.

Walking on, I pass the Roman museum, where outside an actor is dressed as a gladiator in a red tabard and a silver helmet, brandishing a sword. A group of children listen to him intently as he speaks about the Roman occupation in Chester, before they are ushered inside the museum.

Back at the café, I open up just as Sue arrives with her scones and buns.

'I still can't thank you enough for looking after the shop,' I tell her as we place the bakes under various glass domes and I get the café ready for the day.

'I enjoyed every minute of it,' she tells me. 'I really did.'

'You don't fancy buying it, do you?' I ask, only half-joking.

I'd been discussing the move to Greece with Sue, telling her how much I'd love the café to go to someone who will love it as much as I do. In fact, I've talked about it non-stop, and despite Sue's initial shock, she has been nothing but supportive.

'Actually, I've been thinking about it,' she says casually, as she arranges a mound of scones on a large plate.

I'm shocked to hear this.

'You have?'

'Yes. I've realised I need to get out more. If I'm honest I've been lonely since Colin died. Working here whilst you've been away has been wonderful. His insurance payout has been sitting in the bank and I've been wondering what to do with it. Buying this place feels like the perfect thing to do. I think Colin would approve somehow.'

'Oh, Sue, I'd be over the moon if the café went to you, I really would. The customers wouldn't feel like there was such a big change then.'

'I'm sure they'd miss you though,' she says kindly. 'And your cakes. You must give me all your recipes.'

I can hardly believe it. It's true, I'd been worrying about who would buy the café, wondering if they might even turn it into something completely different. And even though it would be none of my business, I selfishly like the idea of the café still being here when I come back home to visit. Just the way it always was, serving up coffee and cake. It isn't even on the market yet, so I feel so happy that Sue has been giving it some thought.

'My mind is made up,' Sue says suddenly. 'Ooh, it's exciting! I'll go and speak to the bank later.' She gives me a hug and I'm thrilled at the prospect of leaving the café in such safe hands. It's one thing I can breathe a sigh of relief over. I just have to shake the feelings of guilt over Noah and Milly.

8

Three months later, we're gathered in Milly's garden for a farewell BBQ. Noah is red-faced after an hour on the bouncy castle with the little boy next door, and is thirstily gulping down his orange juice. I feel a sudden pang as I look at his cute little smiling face. I'm going to miss him so much. And the rest of my family, of course.

Mum and Dad have travelled over for the leaving party today, and our friends are all gathered here too. It's a wonderful day. When I broke the news of our move to my parents, Mum told me with her usual candour that she couldn't bear to live in a country with such high temperatures, and what about lizards and spiders? I suppose I kind of wanted her to say that she would miss me, although maybe having moved away already she's become used to the distance between us.

Dad said he couldn't wait to come over and visit us, but Mum said firmly that it would have to be in the autumn months when it's cooler. She also said she would bring some English tea bags with her, being a staunch fan of 'traditional English food'.

'We've always got Skype,' Dad said with a wink, telling me

that I ought to follow my dreams and live wherever I wanted to. It's what my parents did after all, albeit still in the UK.

Milly suddenly stands on a chair – as elegantly as ever, despite wearing a linen shift dress and heels – and taps a spoon against a glass to gain everyone's attention.

'Thank you all so much for being here today as we say farewell to Jamie and Charlie,' she addresses the crowd confidently. 'I would like to wish them the best of luck in their new venture. I know you're all going to miss them as much as I will.' Her voice cracks for a second and she takes a sip of Prosecco. 'I'm so proud of Charlie and Jamie for going after what they really want,' she continues. 'Charlie has always wowed me with her determination and positive attitude to life.'

I swallow down a lump in my throat. I'm not sure I can listen to any more of this.

'My sister is the most unselfish, big-hearted person I know and I'm certain she has found a lifelong partner in Jamie,' she goes on. 'We'll all miss her, but it's not like they are heading off to Australia. It's only a few hours on a plane. We'll see each other all the time,' she says, positively.

'Yeah, and think of all the free holidays!' someone pipes up and the sound of laughter ripples through the crowd.

'So, I hope you'll all join me in raising a glass to Charlie and Jamie and wish them all the best as they head off for their new life in the sun.'

'To Charlie and Jamie,' everyone says in unison before they break out in a round of applause.

A short while later, Milly beckons me inside and hands me a box. I open it to find a beautiful silver charm bracelet inside, with a cupcake charm attached.

'To remind you of the life you once had here,' she says, and I'm so touched by her thoughtfulness I could cry.

'Oh, Milly, thank you. It's so beautiful but you shouldn't have.'

We have a long hug and when Noah comes over and threads his little fingers through mine, the tears that I've been trying to quell almost spill over, but, somehow, I manage to keep it together. For the briefest of seconds, I wonder if we're doing the right thing. I quickly gather my thoughts and realise I can't let sentiment get in the way of our life's ambitions. Today was bound to be an emotional day. We have a new life in Greece to look forward to!

Pixie has been babysitting regularly for Noah, as Milly's romance with Fireman Sam seems to be progressing nicely, and things are going well at the café with Sue at the helm this past week or so. All of this makes me feel good about everyone being happy and settled without me around. Sue has given Pixie some extra hours too, so her saving up is going quite well by all accounts. I was really touched when some of the café regulars clubbed together and presented me with a bottle of wine and some euros in an envelope.

We said our goodbyes before we got to the airport, as I can't bear airport departures.

Jamie had been so fed up in his workplace, especially after two of his work colleagues had also quit in the past week, that he'd talked non-stop about our plans for the future as we waited for our big day to arrive. Now, settling back into the flight, he's talking about the jobs that will need doing in the house.

'I reckon the pool is the first thing we need to get sorted,' says Jamie excitedly as he glances out of the plane window. We're two hours into our journey and the grey clouds that we left behind at Manchester have already been replaced by clear blue skies.

I think that we need to sort out the rooms we're going to be living in first, but I don't want to burst his bubble right now.

We order a drink and some peanuts from the waitress as the trolley passes.

'I can't wait to have a nice moussaka. Or maybe a mixed meze,' says Jamie, before tucking into a cheese and ham toastie, which isn't quite the same.

It feels strange to be travelling to Crete to begin a new life, and I have to remind myself that we are not heading off on holiday. I can already picture long, sunny days chatting to the locals, dining in pretty restaurants beneath the shade of fig and lemon trees, watching the sun go down and welcoming guests into the holiday annexe, when it's up and running. I'm so looking forward to our adventure. Jamie was right when he said we should do these things whilst we are young. I can't imagine anything worse than living a life filled with regrets and 'if onlys'.

We arrive mid-morning and set our cases down in the house, before wandering around taking in every detail of our new home. I imagine the winter months, with the log fire roaring into life beneath the oak beams in the spacious lounge, the walls currently painted a tired-looking beige. The kitchen probably needs the most work, with its cracked tiles and several of the dark cupboards hanging by their hinges, but the potential for family gatherings, as I cook up a sumptuous chicken *souvlaki*, is clear in my mind. Moving through the hall, with its beautiful black and white tiled floor – that is thankfully intact – we head up the dark wooden staircase, passing the beautiful window on the landing once more, to the upper floor where there are two good-sized bedrooms. Glancing around them, it seems they need little more than a lick of paint and some new light fittings. There's already a bed frame in the main bedroom, so we head to a local furniture store to buy a cheap mattress – which will do until our own arrives from England and can then be a spare bed for visitors – along with a couple of large bean bags to sit on, which the store said they would deliver to us that afternoon.

Our next task is to buy a car. Thankfully, as we are cash buyers, there is no red tape involved and we are able to drive home that very day, in our black Fiat Punto.

Just after two o'clock, we head to the village for a late lunch. We see the local restaurant owner we met on our last trip leaning on a tree chatting to a trio of middle-aged women, and he recognises us at once.

'*Kalispera*. Welcome back. I hope you settle into our village.' He gestures for us to sit down at some tables outside and says something in Greek to one of his young waitresses. She disappears into the restaurant, before appearing with a bottle of red wine and three glasses.

'May I join you in a drink to wish you well and welcome you to our village?'

Red wine isn't really Jamie's drink, but he sips at it good-naturedly and thanks Darius for the welcome.

'So, I guess you have a lot of work to do.' He's sitting opposite us, looking smart in a black polo shirt, white jeans and a pair of designer sunglasses.

'All in good time,' says Jamie. 'Right now, I'm famished.'

'Then luckily there is something we can do about that.' Darius smiles as he hands us each a menu.

'It's a great place,' says Jamie. 'How long have you been here?'

'Ten years. I remember when I first started this restaurant up like it was yesterday,' says Darius. 'It was a lot of hard work. Worth it though, I think. It has the best reputation in the village. Maybe even in the whole of Chania. At least I like to think so.' He winks.

'Your English is really good, where did you learn it?' I ask, intrigued.

'A lot of it from English-speaking tourists over the years. And Google Translate.' He laughs. 'The English they taught in schools was maybe not so good. They taught us A is for apple, or where is the bathroom? That sort of thing.' He laughs again and I can't help thinking it sounds a lot like the French I learnt at school.

On each of our visits the restaurant has been busy and well staffed, yet he seems to be a constant presence, overseeing things.

'It must be nice being the boss, though. You can take time off whenever you feel like it, I imagine.' Jamie has clearly already forgotten how he used to grumble that I rarely took time off from the café in Chester.

Darius looks horrified at the very thought.

'Not too much time. I like to make sure my staff maintain the good standards. If you let standards slip, you are soon out of business.'

A waiter makes a timely appearance just then, brandishing a basket of bread.

'Actually,' says Jamie, as he chews on the soft bread. 'Maybe you could help us find a local tradesman. I can do some of the work myself, but I think the outbuilding will need a professional if we want it to be up to the standard of a holiday let.'

'Or maybe we'll have a couple of glamping pods,' I add, thinking of the huge garden.

Darius looks thoughtful. 'A holiday let, maybe. Many tourists come to the village, but camping pods, perhaps not.' He shakes his head.

'Why not?' asks Jamie.

'Because they often attract groups of young people. Fire pits and late-night parties may not go down so well with the residents in the village,' he tells us honestly.

'I take your point. I never thought about that, thank you,' I reply. 'A holiday annexe it is then.'

'Oh, and regarding your builder: I will speak to my brother,

Kostas.' He stands and excuses himself as the trio of women wave over to gain his attention.

After our late lunch, we grab some cold drinks from a supermarket and stroll back to the house in preparation to unpack some more of our things. Our furniture from the UK will be arriving tomorrow, mainly our huge bed and sofa that cost a fortune, so was worth the cost of the transit. As we approach the front of our new home, we see a couple heading towards our house.

'*Kalispera*! Very good timing.'

A man who looks to be in his sixties, with a head of thick, grey-streaked hair, takes us by surprise, embracing us in a bear hug whilst his petite wife stands next to him smiling. She has pretty dark-brown eyes and her dark hair up in a bun. I can't help thinking what an even-more attractive couple they must have made in their younger days. The man introduces himself as Stelios and his wife as Eleni, who hands me a dish covered with a clean tea towel.

'*Spanakopita*,' says Stelios, and I think about the tasty spinach and feta pie that must be within.

'Oh, how delicious, thank you so much.' I gratefully accept the gift.

'Welcome to our village!' Stelios, a giant of a man with a ready smile, has already followed us inside, whilst Eleni stands in the doorway until I invite her in.

I offer them a cold drink from the fridge, but they both politely decline.

'Today I have things to do. Tomorrow, I help you.' He gestures to the wild garden. 'I will bring my gardening tools.'

'That is, if you would like some help,' adds Eleni diplomatically, raising her eyebrows as she glances at her husband, but smiling all the while.

'Of course! I'd love some help,' Jamie replies gratefully. 'I was actually wondering where to get some gardening tools, as we never really had any use for them back home, living in a flat,' he explains. 'That would be amazing, thanks very much.'

'No problem! I will come bright and early before it gets too hot.'

'*Efcharisto poli*,' I say, hoping I have just said thank you very much.

'*Parakalo*,' he replies, which I know means you're welcome.

'Gosh they're lovely neighbours, aren't they? It will be great if everyone in the village is as friendly as that,' I say to Jamie after they've left. 'We'll soon settle in and make friends.' I suddenly feel even more positive about coming here.

'I know, and it's great that Darius has a brother who can sort the outbuilding, too.'

Later, we drive to a large supermarket and purchase food and all manner of cleaning equipment and paint for decorating. The rest of the day is spent hanging up clothes and lifting the broken tiles in the kitchen and placing them in a cardboard box. I give the lounge walls a fresh lick of paint whilst Jamie secures a couple of the kitchen cabinet doors that are hanging off by their hinges. We're hoping to just change the dark brown, slightly old-fashioned-looking doors as the units themselves are fine. The fairly modest-sized kitchen can be opened up with white units and maybe a slightly sparkly worktop. I'm hoping to inject some modern touches that will blend seamlessly with the features, such as the oak beams in the lounge and the solid wooden doors and staircase.

After sweeping the floor, I take the box of broken terracotta tiles outside ready to be disposed of when I notice a pair of beady eyes staring at me from the roof of the outbuilding, and jump in surprise.

'Good grief, how did that get up there?'

Jamie joins me outside and laughs as he sees a black goat

with a white beard standing on the roof of the outbuilding opposite.

'It's a mountain goat. They like climbing onto high things. I did see some on the surrounding hills on the journey in, but I never expected they would venture into the garden.' Jamie smiles, seemingly unperturbed by its presence.

'Shoo, go away, Billy.' I waft a tea towel in its general direction as the animal continues to stare straight through me, unmoved.

'Billy? That's a bit unimaginative, isn't it?'

'Got a better name? I can't believe I'm discussing possible goat names!'

'Scape?'

'What?'

'Duh. Scape goat.'

'Oh, very funny.' I roll my eyes.

'Anyway, you're wasting your time here.' Jamie seems to find the whole situation amusing. 'You know why it's so hard to have a conversation with a goat, don't you?'

'No, why?'

'Because they're always *butting* in.' He laughs at his own joke and I lash him with the tea towel.

That evening, we enjoy a slice of the delicious *spanakopita* with a cold beer, seated outside in the covered patio area. It's lovely to have a shady place outside, a respite from the searing summer heat.

After our supper I stare out at the jungle of the garden and imagine how wonderful it could be. I'm visualising some pots bursting with colourful plants in the future and a nice dining set – the metal one we are currently sitting at is slightly rusty with a wonky table leg. Some solar lights dotted about would look great, too, and a neat lawn. Maybe even a raised bed somewhere to grow beetroots and lettuce for salads, along with rosemary and oregano growing along the borders. Perhaps a lavender bush too!

I head inside feeling tired and all too ready for bed, but with a real sense of enthusiasm for the project that lies ahead of us. We're really going to make our dream happen.

9

I awake the next morning to the sound of whistling coming from outside. The stand-up fan in the corner did little to venti-late the room last night, even with the window flung open, although admittedly we were so tired that we both slept like the dead. The whistling sound is suddenly replaced by singing, so I groggily glance at the clock on the bedside table. It's seven o'clock.

I grab a robe and peek out of the bedroom window to see Stelios pulling weeds and piling them into a wheelbarrow.

'*Kalimera!*' I shout down.

'*Kalimera*, how are you?' He lifts his hand and waves.

'Good, thank you. I'll be down in just a minute.'

The sun is already bathing the green lawn in a glorious morning sheen.

I nudge Jamie and tell him that Stelios is downstairs making a start on the garden.

'What?' He rubs his eyes. 'It's a bit early to be gardening, surely?'

'I'll go down and get the coffee on. See you in a minute.' I quickly slip into a T-shirt and shorts, ready to head downstairs as Jamie attempts to roll over. I pull the white cotton sheet from him and he grumbles as I leave to make the coffee.

'Good morning, Stelios.' I carry a pot of coffee outside, along with some cold bottled water and set it on the table.

'Hello. I hope I did not wake you. I was waiting until you were up before I begin with the lawnmower.' He grins broadly, so I don't have the heart to tell him that his loud whistling woke me from my slumber.

Jamie appears ten minutes later, wiping the telltale crumbs of a Danish pastry from his mouth.

The two men set about clearing the garden, Jamie bending and stretching as he pulls at weeds, Stelios happily mowing the lawn, singing an unfamiliar Greek tune as he works. Jamie tackles some spreading vines with the secateurs and a couple of hours later it's already beginning to look like less of a wilderness.

'I think that is enough for one day.' Stelios wipes sweat from his forehead with a handkerchief, before heading to an outdoor tap where he washes his hands and splashes water over his face.

'Thank you so much for today, Stelios. The garden is looking so different already,' I tell him, gratefully.

I glance at the white picket fence that separates the garden from the olive grove, still hardly able to believe that it belongs to us.

'Those olives,' says Stelios, following my gaze. 'I will ask someone to come and take a look,' he offers. 'See if they are ready to harvest. Unless, of course, you plan on harvesting them yourselves?'

It's not something Jamie or I would consider doing, not knowing the first thing about picking olives, so it makes sense for someone else to do the work. 'Thanks again, I don't know how to repay you,' I say, wondering if I will offend him if I offer him some money.

'You are my new neighbours: I am happy to help. Too long

this house has stood empty. I am happy to know that new life is being breathed back into it. So is my wife,' he tells us in his strong Greek accent.

As Stelios leaves, the sound of a truck rumbling along the quiet road can be heard. Our furniture arriving from England! Several hours later, having scrubbed and cleaned everything from the floor tiles to the windows, everything is in place and we stand back and admire our new home.

The lounge looks cosy and inviting, with an open brick fireplace and a pair of new curtains in a soft grey. The white walls that I painted yesterday have given the room a fresh, clean look and our red rug from home looks perfect in front of the fireplace giving the room a welcoming feel. Once the cracked window-pane has been replaced and the frames spruced up with a new lick of paint, it should look even better. Hopefully Darius's brother, Kostas, will be able to help us sort that out too.

'Right, I think we're done here.' Jamie checks his watch. 'Do you fancy driving into Chania for a late lunch?'

We have a fridge full of food, but I guess a trip to Chania does sound rather nice, and I imagine a walk along the harbour would be very pleasant on a beautiful day like today.

We're about to leave when a balding, middle-aged man steps out of a blue car and heads towards our gate.

'*Kalimera*. My name is Manos. I come to take a look at your olives?' he informs us.

'Oh, yes, hi.' I'm surprised at how quickly he has arrived as I welcome him into the garden.

I open a gate in the white picket fence and lead him into the olive grove. He moves from tree to tree, quietly inspecting the olives and assessing their quality.

'Yes,' he says eventually. 'I think half, maybe three quarters, of your olives are good. Perhaps they will all be even better next year, with some careful pruning.' He nods his head thoughtfully.

He explains that he can take them in October and turn them into olive oil at his local factory. He'll then give us some of the bottles to keep.

'That sounds wonderful, thank you.'

'Sometimes people in the village swap their produce,' he tells us. 'A bottle of olive oil for some tomatoes or aubergines.'

'What a lovely idea.' I imagine it could be a good way to make friends, too.

Manos takes our contact details and heads off, then we continue as planned with our journey into Chania.

10

The harbour is bustling when we arrive, the sand-coloured buildings bathed in sunlight, the sun glistening on the gorgeous sea. Diners are seated outside restaurants overlooking the harbour, as waiters buzz about serving them plates of delicious-looking food. Strolling past an impressive old mosque, the building now used as an art gallery, we head inside. We browse lots of beautiful paintings and eventually purchase two seascapes in striking watercolours that will look good on the white-painted walls of our newly decorated lounge.

On a cobbled street on the harbour front we find an outdoor table at a restaurant overlooking the water. After dining on melt-in-the-mouth lamb *kleftico*, followed by ice cream, we explore the winding, narrow streets, many of the shops housed in white buildings with traditional blue-painted doors. Passing a stand displaying bags outside a shop, my hands run over a soft, red leather shoulder bag at a bargain price.

'Go on, you know you want it,' urges Jamie.

I feel a little guilty buying the bag, especially as the house still needs so much money spent on it, but with Jamie's encouragement I head inside to pay. The shop is so narrow that two teenage boys who are looking at Converse backpacks have to press themselves against a wall to let me get past. Once I've paid, I place my old bag in the carrier bag from the shop, and pull my new purchase onto my shoulder.

'Where to now?' asks Jamie as we walk along contentedly.

'How about a walk to the lighthouse?' I suggest.

We hold hands as we stroll along and I have to pinch myself for a minute that we're actually living here in Crete. This is our life now! We watch boats speeding across the waves in the distance; one filled with tourists glides along the blue green water. I can hardly wait to welcome visitors to our annexe, greeting them with cakes and freshly made bread.

It's almost seven o'clock when we arrive home and bump into Stelios, who is wearing a Greek football shirt and making his way to a local bar to watch a match. He asks Jamie if he would like to join him. Jamie doesn't need to be asked twice, so they head off together and I walk outside into the garden, pulling some lemons from a tree. It feels so wonderful to just be able to pull fresh lemons with such intense flavour from the tree here. I've already made lemonade, which is super quick and easy, and I decide that tonight I'm going to make a lemon drizzle cake.

Squeezing the fresh lemon juice and beating the cake batter reminds me of just how much I love to bake. Once the cake is out of the oven, cooled and drizzled with lemon syrup, I wrap some in greaseproof paper and take it across to Eleni.

'Charlotte, *kalispera*.' She welcomes me inside her home, the lounge painted in a pale yellow contrasting perfectly with the traditional Greek dark-wooden furniture. Photographs are displayed on walls, and dozens of books line a tall, narrow wooden bookcase. The stone floor is made cosy with a large Persian-style rug in shades of orange, creams and gold.

Eleni thanks me for the cake and makes a pot of tea and, as

it's still warm, we take it outside and sit at a wooden table with two benches beneath a canopy. The long garden is mainly flagged and filled with colourful flowers in glazed pots and has a large shed at the end. Eleni pours the tea before she takes a mouthful of the cake.

'Oh my goodness, this is delicious. You bake like a professional.'

'Maybe that's because I am,' I say, telling her all about my little café back home in Chester.

'There was once a bakery near the school but it closed down. The cakes in the supermarket are just not the same,' she tells me, which gives me food for thought.

I decide to ask Eleni about the previous tenants of the house, as Darius had revealed that the owner had lost his wife.

'Yes.' Her eyes suddenly mist over. 'Athena was my best friend.'

'I'm so sorry. You must miss her,' I say gently.

'Every day. We liked to talk and have tea every morning when our chores were done. Sometimes, we would take long walks or go shopping into Chania. I miss her sense of fun,' she says, the memory clearly tugging at her heartstrings. 'She should never have died the way she did. Her life was cut short.' A flicker of anger crosses her face as she stands. 'Would you like some more tea?' she asks, signalling that the conversation about her friend is over, for now at least.

'No, thank you. I suppose I ought to be getting back. I feel bad sitting around for too long when there are still so many things to do in the house.'

'Thank you so much for the cake. I'm sure Stelios will enjoy some when he comes home.'

Half an hour later, I'm yawning as Jamie comes through the door and I hear the voice of Stelios wishing him goodnight.

'Did you enjoy that?' I ask as he spies a slice of lemon cake on the kitchen counter and stuffs half of it into his mouth.

'It was great. Mmm, so is this. I've missed your baking! Anyway, Stelios was telling me about a sports centre a couple of miles from here. I think we passed it on our way, do you remember? The football pitches were inside some metal fences.'

'Yes, I think I do.'

'Well, they play every Tuesday and Friday, just like back home.' Jamie's full of enthusiasm and I know it will be something that will help him to settle here.

'Let's hope they all speak English then.'

'It doesn't matter if they don't. Football is a universal language. Anyway, let's get to bed and give that goat something to gawp at,' says Jamie, guiding me upstairs.

'What? It's not there again, is it?'

'Yup. On the roof of the outbuilding.'

'Well, remember to draw the curtains. And close the window. Although it will probably get a little hot in bed.'

'It certainly will,' says Jamie as he pulls me in for a kiss.

11

The following morning, I take an early walk around the village. It's so nice to head out before the sun really gets up. I notice a few of the locals are beginning to recognise me as I stroll past, calling out 'kalimera' from their gardens, as they head off for work or hang out the day's washing. Most of the work is done in the morning here, especially in the summer months to avoid the intense midday heat. Even school seems to start and finish earlier than at home. The thought of school suddenly reminds me of Noah and gives me a little stab to the heart.

At the top end of the village, near the school and the unused bakery, is a bar with an outside area covered by a straw roof. It's mainly frequented by the locals, as opposed to the tavernas and bars on the main street that attract tourists during the summer months, as Stelios informed me yesterday.

After popping into the small supermarket for a bottle of iced tea, I sit on a circular wall outside the playground that has a large fig tree at its centre. A few minutes later, a young woman with flowing dark, curly hair comes rushing past accompanied by two young boys.

The younger one, who looks about five, runs towards the

swings in the play area, followed by the slightly older-looking boy and the woman calling after them in Greek.

'*Kalimera.*' I smile at the woman.

'Hello, *kalimera.*' She hurriedly follows the children. The older boy is already climbing up the slide when suddenly I hear a loud squeal as the younger child has slid off the swing and fallen onto his knees. The woman rushes towards him, dabbing at his legs with a tissue she has quickly retrieved from her bag.

I rush over, pull some plasters from my new shoulder bag and offer her one. I'd got into a habit of carrying them around with me from when I looked after Noah.

'*Efcharisto*, thank you,' she says, applying the sticking plaster that is decorated with pictures of robots onto the grazed knee of the child. The crying quickly stops.

'We should not even be here. The children are late for school, but they always run ahead of me.' She sighs.

I introduce myself and she tells me her name is Katerina. 'But my friends call me Kat.'

'I'm Charlotte, but my friends call me Charlie.'

'*Ella, ella.*' She gestures to the older boy, who is just about to climb up the slide for a second time. He pulls a face but does as he is told.

'You have beautiful children,' I say, looking at their cute faces with large, deep brown eyes.

'Oh they are not my children.' She smiles. 'It is my job to take them to school and collect them, then watch them for a few hours until one of their parents returns from work. I trained as a baker here in the village, so this is not my dream job, but it pays well,' she reveals, smiling once more. 'I really must go, the children are already so late,' she says, glancing at her watch. 'This playground is too much of a temptation in the morning. Goodbye, Charlie.'

She holds the boys firmly by the hand and they hurry off.

I take a circular walk, passing the restaurants on the main

street where the owners are setting up tables outside for breakfast and beeping trucks are negotiating the narrow roads as they
make deliveries of food and drink.

Darius is standing outside his restaurant talking to someone
as I walk past.

'*Kalimera!*' He ends his conversation with the man and
heads towards me. 'Are you home today? My brother Kostas
tells me he can come and take a look at your outbuilding around
two o'clock. He will give you a price for the work.'

'That would be perfect! Thank you so much.'

He nods before heading back to the man to resume their
conversation. I take a proper look at the main street that we
passed in the car yesterday. It's lined with trees and the bars and
restaurants are interspersed with a beauty salon, a supermarket
and a gift shop that has postcards displayed on stands outside,
along with fridge magnets and souvenirs. There is also a shop
that offers cars and quad bikes for hire, the vehicles displayed in
a car park adjacent to the shop. The village has everything we
need, although there is the large supermarket a short drive
away too.

I head home feeling energised after my walk, ready to do
some more painting. Jamie has surfaced now and is sitting on
the outside terrace drinking coffee.

'You were up early,' he remarks as he pours me a coffee. 'I
thought I might have worn you out last night.' He lifts his arms
above his head and yawns.

'I've always been an early riser, and since having the café...
well!'

'So have I. But it's still a pity you went out so early,' he adds
cheekily.

I tell him all about Kostas coming over later to take a look at
the outbuilding when I hear the unmistakeable sound of Stelios
whistling as he strides purposefully across the garden.

'Are you ready for another morning's work?' he asks Jamie.

He's raring to go with his sleeves rolled up on his light blue shirt and a smile on his face. 'Here, these are for you.' He hands me a carrier bag of tomatoes. 'My tomatoes have grown like crazy this year.'

'Thank you, Stelios, that is so kind.'

It reminds me to buy some terracotta pots, find a sunny spot in the garden and have a go at growing my own.

'*Kalimera*, Stelios.' Jamie downs his coffee. 'Yep, I'm ready to work, but I think I need one more coffee first.' Jamie offers Stelios one, but he declines.

'I have espresso in the morning. One.' He holds a single finger up. 'The rest of the day, I drink water, important in this heat especially when you are working. When I finish my work, I have one more espresso. But never in the evening, or I stay awake all night bothering my wife.' He lets out a loud laugh that is impossible not to join him in.

The men work hard in the garden, taking regular water breaks, and Stelios asks if I have any more lemon cake, telling me it was delicious and that it will keep him going. I whip up a batch of scones, as they are so quick to make. Forty minutes later, I serve them with butter and strawberry jam and, though I say so myself, they taste especially good – maybe it's the ingredients here.

We're just enjoying another break – Stelios raving about the scones – when a good-looking man with closely cropped hair, wearing a navy vest that displays his tattooed arms, steps out of a truck. As he walks closer, I can't help noticing his eyes are a deep hazel colour.

'*Kalispera*. My name is Kostas, I am here to take a look at some possible building work.'

'Good afternoon, Kostas, thank you for coming.'

'And you arrive at just the right time,' Stelios says, pushing a scone under his nose.

'Hmm, tempting. They look very good, but I don't eat

cakes.' Observing his flat stomach and muscular arms, this comes as no surprise.

'Okay, well I'll lead the way.' I smile brightly as I guide Kostas to the neglected white stone building at the edge of the garden.

He pushes and prods the walls, examining the floor and the rotting window frames. Soon his inspection of the property is finished.

'There is a little damp that will need looking at and you will need new windows and flooring. But the building itself is solid. I will be able to fix it up. Are you going to rent it out?' he asks, as I walk him to his truck.

I tell him our plans to turn it into a one-bedroomed holiday let as we discuss adding a bathroom and small kitchen.

'Which should attract couples,' I add. 'I thought it might appeal to hikers and nature lovers. I heard there are some pretty walking trails locally.'

'Yes, it is a good area for walking,' he agrees. 'Lake Agia is beautiful as well, with lots of outdoor tables for a picnic. A nice restaurant too, as I recall, surrounded by the forest.'

'That sounds lovely, I'll remember that.'

Kostas tells me he will draw up some proper plans, but for now he roughly sketches an outline of the work on a pad he takes from a side pocket in his black cargo trousers. The price he suggests is more than fair, and will still leave a healthy amount of money in the bank, so I accept his quote and offer him the job. He says he'll be back tomorrow morning to get started on the prep work and bids me goodbye.

When Stelios and Jamie are finishing up, Jamie tells him he wishes we had a pool that he could dive right into.

'You want a pool built?' Stelios asks as he packs some gardening tools away.

'Yeah, we need to find someone to do it. It's hard to know who is going to be reliable, as well as give a good price. Do you know anyone?' Jamie asks hopefully.

'Of course! You are looking at him.' He puffs his chest out. 'I will do it for a very fair price.'

Jamie and I exchange a look.

'Ah, I know what you think,' says Stelios. 'You think I am an old man. But my son, Apollo, will be home soon from university for the summer holidays. He will help me. We had him late in life so he will be the muscle and I the brains. I am sure he will be glad of the chance to earn a little money.'

'Have you built a pool before?' I ask him curiously.

'But of course! Not for many years, but it's not something you forget.'

Stelios tells us he will have it done by the end of the summer, which sounds fantastic. A pool would definitely be an attractive feature if we do rent out the annexe, so it's really an investment as much as for our own pleasure. We can hardly believe how kind the locals have been and the work estimates are far less than we could ever have imagined. With a few calculations we work out there will still be some money left in the bank after the renovations, although we know we need to be generating an income soon, as it won't last for long.

Heading inside, I remember Milly is going to call me this afternoon, and just after four o'clock I'm peering at her smiling face across a computer screen.

'Charlotte, hi! How's things?'

'Milly, it's so good to see you.' We start chatting when Noah comes bounding over into full view of the camera.

'Hi, Auntie Charlie!'

'Hey, Noah, what are you up to?' Looking at my cute nephew, with his blond ruffled hair, brings a smile to my face.

'I've just been making a speedboat with my Lego. We're going out later on a real boat,' he tells me excitedly. He runs to get his Lego boat and proudly shows it to me, moving it up and down as if on the waves.

'Oh wow, that's brilliant. Maybe when you come here you can go out in a boat on the sea, would you like that?'

'Yeah.' He runs off to his Lego, with a 'bye', and Milly and I resume our chat.

She tells me things are going well with Sam and that she's thinking about introducing him to Noah.

'Up until now, Pixie has looked after Noah here and there when I've gone out to meet Sam. She's a great girl and has been a lifeline for me. Anyway, Noah has been asking me about the "friend" I sometimes go out to see. I just wanted to be sure he was a nice man first, but it's been a few months now.'

'Sounds sensible. So do you think he might be the one?'

'I really hope so. It took me a long time to build up trust after Dan but I can't let that scar me. I like being in a relationship with him. He's so lovely, Charlie, I know you'll really like him when you get to know him properly.'

'I'm sure I will.'

He appeared briefly at the leaving BBQ and introductions were made, but he couldn't stay long as he had a shift at the fire station later. He mingled with the crowd and Milly made a point of not introducing him to Noah.

'Anyway, I'm counting the weeks until Noah and I come and visit you!' she says excitedly. 'I can't wait to see you and Jamie and spend a whole week in the sun. It will still be sunny in October, won't it?' She laughs.

'I'm told it's still warm at that time of year, yes. It will be nice for Noah to have a half-term holiday too, before he heads back to school. Aw, I can't wait to see you both.'

The sun is so hot in July and August, Milly decided to wait and bring Noah along in October, which makes sense as I'm told there was a heatwave here last August when the temperature broke all records.

'Are you sure you'll be able to tear yourself away from Sam?' I tease.

'Well, they do say absence makes the heart grow fonder. I guess it will reveal how I really feel about him.'

I tell her that there is the possibility we will have a pool built by the time they arrive, but not to mention it to Noah in case it isn't finished.

'Ooh, how exciting. It sounds like it's all systems go. I'm so proud of you, sis.'

'I'm proud of you too,' I tell her.

We chat for a while longer, and blow kisses to each other when we finish the conversation and I feel so happy when I walk back into the garden, where Jamie is sitting at the table drinking cold lemonade.

'I think I might head over to that football pitch later if that's okay, see if I can get a game in,' Jamie says.

'Of course, but I thought you'd be exhausted after all your hard work in the garden.'

'Football relaxes me. I miss not having a good kick about. Maybe I'll have a bit of a siesta first though.'

He heads inside and I prepare some salad using the tomatoes that Stelios gave us, before I nip to the local supermarket to buy some feta. I'm going to make a quiche to eat with the salad later. One day, I'll think about maybe sectioning a small area of the land for hens, to have my own eggs, as many of the villagers do.

I knock at Eleni's to ask if she would like anything from the shop and, remembering what Manos said about exchanging gifts, I bring some scones as a thank you for the tomatoes. There's no answer at the front door, so I walk around the side of the house where I can see her sitting in the garden drinking a cup of tea. I think I hear her quietly sob, so I discreetly walk away, wondering what my new friend could be crying about.

12

Jamie returns at about nine in the evening, in a good mood having enjoyed his game of football with the locals, telling me they were a decent bunch of lads who made him feel very welcome.

'One of the players there is world class. Honestly, he makes Ronaldo look like an amateur. Seven goals he scored. So glad he was on my team.' He laughs.

It makes me think of the evenings he would return with a takeaway after his football matches back in Chester. Instead, we take the quiche and salad and eat outside, catching the last of the sun's rays. It's so beautiful and peaceful watching the sun go down and hearing the sound of the crickets in the hedgerows.

'I've got something to tell you.' I'd just finished a phone call with Steph before he arrived home.

'What's that then?'

'Well, it was going to be a surprise, but I know you don't like those, and I'm rubbish at keeping secrets anyway. Besides, we'd have to go and pick them up.'

'What? Who? Don't leave me hanging here,' he says, with the excitement of a small child.

'Matty and Steph.'

'What about them?'

'They're coming over to stay at the end of the month!'

'That's the best news ever!' he says, punching the air. 'It's a pity the annexe isn't fixed up, but never mind, we have two bedrooms, I suppose.' He's grinning wildly. 'How long are they staying for?'

'A week. Steph wasn't sure she could get the time off at short notice, but she's put in a lot of extra hours lately, so her boss was fine about it.'

'We'll need to sort the guest room then.'

'Yep. Looks like a trip to Chania for some new bedding. Oh, and a new floor lamp. I can't wait for them to get here!'

Truthfully, I hadn't expected our friends would come until later in the year, but I really can't wait to see them. I miss Steph and how she makes me laugh. We have regular phone chats but it's not quite the same. It's going to be so wonderful spending time together again, and I can't wait to show her the best places in Chania. Milly and Noah will be over soon too, so there is a lot to look forward to already.

Kostas arrives just after seven thirty the next morning wearing black shorts and a khaki vest, just as I am making coffee downstairs.

'*Kalimera*. I hope I am not too early?' he asks, probably noting that I'm still wearing my robe.

'No, of course not. I imagine you start early because of the heat?' I hand him a coffee.

'Yes, I finish around two o'clock, when the sun is at its hottest. Although, I have a few small jobs to finish up elsewhere after here, so no rest for me today.'

He smiles and although he has a slightly different build and hairstyle, I can definitely see the resemblance to his brother, Darius.

He takes his coffee across to the annexe, so I leave him to it and head upstairs to get dressed, before busying myself with some chores around the house. Shortly afterwards, a delivery of new sand-coloured quarry tiles arrives. They will look lovely against the new cream kitchen doors that will replace the old ones. Jamie sets about laying the tiles, a skill his father taught him, so I finish the final coat of paint on the kitchen walls. As I'm working, I notice a watermark across the ceiling and hope it's nothing to be concerned about. Maybe I'll ask Kostas to take a look at it some time.

Stelios appears a while later with his tape measure, singing to himself as he measures an area in the vast garden.

'I'm not sure it's a good idea having two workmen here at the same time,' I say to Jamie. 'The place will be a building site when Matty and Steph come over.'

'That's true, although I can't imagine work on the pool would start so soon. Stelios will need to order the materials. Even so, I'll give him the heads-up.'

After a chat with Jamie in the garden, Stelios agrees to begin the work after our guests leave.

'Actually,' says Jamie. 'Why don't we just get one of those above ground pools for now, and see how we find that instead? It could be up and erected in time for Matty and Steph arriving. Some of them look pretty decent.'

'Jamie, that's a brilliant idea! It's something I would never have thought of.'

'And it will save a load of money,' he adds.

'You're right.'

'Up here for thinking,' – he taps his head – 'down there for dancing.' He points at his feet, and I laugh.

I head over to see Stelios immediately, to inform him that our plans have changed. He gives me the impression he's someone who likes to have a project to think about and may already be sourcing materials for the pool so I don't want him to be disappointed.

Stelios smiles good-naturedly when I decline his offer of building a pool and asks if I would like him to build us an outdoor sauna instead, which makes me laugh.

'So, with all the money we're saving, I say we eat out in the village this evening,' Jamie suggests when I return.

'Why not?' I tell Jamie. 'An evening out sounds good. We're making good progress with the house after all.'

Later that evening, we head to a different restaurant in the village, which, although pretty good, we both agree isn't as enjoyable as The Fig Tree. Afterwards, we head to a local bar, which is busy, with live music being played. The old, terracotta-coloured brick building has tables outside in a courtyard beneath trees with lights threaded through the branches. A group of people are leaving an outside table, and a waiter appears in a flash and clears it, so we sit down and order.

As we sit chatting and sipping our drinks, a group of four English people at the next table strike up a conversation with us. They are from the North of England and tell us they are here on holiday.

'We're getting a bus into Platanias soon,' says one of the women, who has cropped black hair and a wide smile. 'It's lovely here, but a little quiet. We go home in two days so we want to sample as much of the Platanias nightlife as we can before we leave.'

Her friends agree and one of the blokes in the group asks us if we fancy joining them. I'm pretty pooped after our day's work, but I can see that Jamie is raring to go.

'It's only around a ten-minute walk,' Jamie tells the group.

'In these shoes? No chance,' laughs a blonde female, pointing to her sky-high wedges.

'What do you think?' Jamie looks at me hopefully. 'It is Saturday night after all.'

'I suppose it is. Go on then.'

Jamie looks thrilled and when we finish our drinks, we all head to the bus stop across the road, sitting on a low white-painted wall, chatting.

'I can't believe you actually live here,' says one of the blokes. 'That's gotta be a dream come true.'

'Early days yet, mate. We've got a lot to do in the house, but so far so good,' Jamie says positively.

Ten minutes later the bus arrives and soon enough we are walking along Platanias high street. The sky is turning pink as we walk, a buzz in the air as music pumps from bars and neon lights beckon us towards them. The hum of rides from a children's fairground fills the air, the smell of hot dogs and popcorn reaching our nostrils.

One of the group consults the map on her phone, and directs us down a side street, leading away from the high street towards the beach. A couple are strolling along the sand, the woman carrying her sandals. Suddenly they stop and face each other, to steal a lingering kiss. I smile as I recall the early days of our relationship, when Jamie and I would stop and do the same thing, as we walked home from an evening out along the banks of the River Dee. There's nothing like young love.

We follow the group, and a few minutes later we are approaching an outdoor bar with bamboo chairs and huge pot plants.

'The cocktails here are amazing! And cheaper than on the main street,' says Carrie, the girl with the cropped hair. 'Maybe one here and then on to a cool Scandi bar we discovered a few days ago?'

'Sounds amazing. We haven't had time to explore the nightlife yet, so it's great to have some tips.'

We down strawberry daiquiris and mojitos, watching the waves gently lap the shore as the sky begins to darken. It's so beautiful here that I'd be happy to stay all evening, being lulled by the sound of the sea, but I sense the others are ready for a dance, as they are already tapping their feet along to the music.

We finish our drinks and a few minutes later we head to a building with a smart front door and a couple of steel tables and chairs outside.

The Scandinavian-style bar has cool, clean lines, white tables with curved edges and chunky chairs. A waitress is carrying delicious-looking cocktails towards a table and, inside a booth, a DJ is playing music. The dance floor is illuminated by blue light, creating shadows of the people dancing. It's not the place for conversation, so we order a drink before heading to the dance floor, letting our hair down and dancing the night away.

At the end of a really enjoyable evening, we stroll towards a taxi rank, chattering away, me feeling slightly tipsy but happy. I'm glad Jamie persuaded me to head out of the village for the evening; it's the first time I've really let off steam in a while. We split off into two taxis, wishing the gang an enjoyable time for the remaining few days of their holiday.

'And next year we will have our own accommodation up for rent,' I declare with certainty, although judging by their earlier comments that the village is a little quiet for them, maybe it's not the type of place the group would be interested in holidaying at again.

When we finally arrive home, I think I see the shadow of a man in the distance walking through the olive grove. I ask Jamie if he noticed anything and he says no, but we walk along anyway to investigate. There's no one there.

'How many have you had?' he asks jokingly. 'Goats and now people that disappear into thin air.'

'You've seen the goat yourself, so I know I'm not going mad,' I remind him and he laughs.

I know how easily shadows can fool you, playing tricks with the light, especially in the evening. Even so, I double check the doors and close the curtains firmly before I climb into bed. As Jamie takes me in his arms and kisses me, I quickly put it out of my mind.

13

Kostas is already making great strides with the outbuilding, arriving early and working relentlessly, stopping only briefly for refreshment. A small kitchen and bathroom have been fitted, and tomorrow the new floor will be laid and new windows installed.

I'm heading over with some iced tea for him and a slice of homemade quiche, when I'm sure I see the mysterious figure lurking again in the olive groves. I ask Kostas if he has noticed anything in the bushes or the grove and he shrugs his shoulders.

'No, only the occasional goat. Oh, and the odd snake.' He takes a bite of his quiche and declares it 'very tasty'.

'Excuse me? What did you say?' I stare at him in disbelief.

'It is very tasty.'

'No, rewind to the snake bit.'

'They are only leopard snakes. Don't worry about it, they are harmless,' he tells me casually. 'Besides, they are quite rare,' he adds, maybe after seeing the look of horror on my face. 'Also, from time to time, you may see a cat snake. They do have venom, but it is very weak, you will come to no harm.'

'Can we stop with the snakes?' I plead.

'Sure, sorry.' He takes another bite of the quiche and makes an appreciative noise.

There is no way I am ever setting foot in that olive grove again, even if the snakes are harmless.

We're having the above ground pool delivered today and I can hardly wait. It will be so lovely to have something to cool off in, especially after a day of working on the house, just relaxing in the garden, chatting and sunbathing. I'm going to thread some lights through the trees, as well as install the solar lighting, for cosy, intimate evenings spent outdoors. In the cooler months, we can install some patio heaters so we can sit and watch the moonlight.

Later that day, when the pool has been erected and filled, we change into our swimming things and jump right in, enjoying some respite from the searing heat.

'This is the life, hey?' I swim up next to Jamie, and he takes me in his arms and kisses me.

'It sure is, although I can't get over the fact that this is our actual home. I keep thinking I'm on a long holiday.' He lies on his back and stares up at the sun blazing in a brilliant blue sky.

'Well, it is, so you'd better get used to it!' I splash him with water and he grabs me and tickles me, sending me into fits of giggles.

After our swim, we have to finish our chores for the day. I take pride in sweeping the new floor in the kitchen and running my hand along the granite worktop with the flecks of sparkle.

Noticing a huge cobweb in a corner of the hall, I attack it with a brush, when the biggest spider I've ever seen plops onto the floor and races towards me at full speed. Jamie appears from the garden after hearing my scream and bursts into laughter when he discovers the reason why.

'It's not funny. It was the size of a tarantula,' I tell him as my heart races. 'And more importantly, where is it now?'

Jamie spots it in a corner. Cupping it with his hands, he takes it outside to dispose of it somewhere.

'Ugh, you could have used a glass and a piece of cardboard.' I shudder and he laughs again, telling me that they don't bite.

'Or at least I don't think they do. I don't know much about Greek spiders. That's enough work for one day anyway. Shall we go for a drink after dinner?'

'Deal.' I place the broom back in a cupboard and give a little shudder.

I suggest visiting the bar at the top of the village after we've eaten, which is mainly frequented by the village residents.

'I think it will be a good way to get to know the locals,' I say as I enter the bedroom, having just stepped out of the shower. Jamie is on his phone looking at some sports news, complaining about the slow Wi-Fi.

'What? Yeah, okay, that sounds good,' he says, sounding mildly irritated.

'I don't suppose everything can be perfect,' I say, referring to the slow internet.

'Maybe the bar will have a better connection,' he says optimistically.

Jamie griddles some steaks on the BBQ, along with some halloumi and serves it with a salad, before we head off to the village bar, a little after seven o'clock.

'I bet Matty and Steph will be going into town tonight,' says Jamie as we walk along. 'I can't wait until they come to stay, they can fill us in on all the gossip.'

'Well, you only have a few days to wait.' I thread my arm through his as we walk along in the balmy evening. One or two people that I recognise from my morning walks are out with their dogs and wish us a good evening as we pass.

'You know lots of people here already,' comments Jamie as we stroll on.

'I wouldn't say I know them exactly, but I recognise them

from my walks around the village, before you even surface,' I explain. 'Maybe you could join me some mornings.'

'Maybe.' He shrugs.

We enter the bar, which is painted cream and simply furnished with wooden tables and chairs. The walls display some black-and-white photos of the village in days gone by and I recognise a picture of the huge fig tree that stands outside the school. As we approach the bar, the unmistakeable voice of Stelios and his laughter rings out. He raises his arms in the air when he spots us, and calls us over to join them. Eleni is sitting next to him sipping an ouzo with ice in a tall, thin glass. Stelios is wearing a bright orange shirt with pictures of dancers on it, and Eleni looks elegant in a white cotton dress.

'My friends! Here, here.'

Someone pulls another table over to make one long one and Stelios introduces us to several people including the bar owner, Pepe. There are two blokes around the same age as Jamie, and a couple who look to be in their sixties: a woman with soft grey hair in a bob and a bald man with a cheerful, smiling face. Two old men wearing flat caps are engrossed in a game of dominoes at a table further away, but they lift their hands and smile when Stelios shouts over to them and introduces us.

'It's so nice to see you here this evening. This is a place to have a proper conversation, not like the bars on the main street, with their loud music.'

I can't help noticing that there isn't even a television to watch sport here.

We order some drinks from the bar and Pepe sets cold beers down in front of us, along with a bowl of peanuts, welcoming us to his establishment.

'I was just telling my friends,' says Stelios, holding court with the people around the table, 'about the problem I had with parking when I went into Chania today.'

'It can get really busy,' I agree.

'That's something I don't miss about living in a city,' says Jamie, taking a sip of his beer.

'Yes, yes. Anyway, I wait for a few minutes, when a space becomes free. Suddenly a local vicar dives into the space from right under my nose. I say to him, with respect, Father, you have stolen my parking space.'

'That is annoying,' says Jamie, shaking his head.

'And do you know what he says?' Stelios asks his captive audience.

Everyone shakes their heads.

'He says, I park in this very same spot every single day. And so I say to him...' He pauses for a moment as he sips his ouzo. 'Okay, I can see you are a *preacher* of habit. Haha!'

The table erupts in laughter.

'You had me there for a minute,' says Jamie.

'You can never be sure if Stelios is telling the truth or joking,' says one of the younger blokes. Suddenly I'm slightly relieved I never actually agreed to him building a pool, wondering whether his claim of building pools before was a bit of a bluff.

'Talking of cars,' says Jamie. 'Did you read about that bloke who made a car out of spaghetti?'

'Spaghetti? Never,' answers Stelios, shaking his head.

'Well, his wife didn't believe him ether, until he drove right pasta.'

The uproarious laughter continues and Stelios slaps Jamie on the back in delight. 'I like it! I will remember that one!'

We spend the next couple of hours chatting and learning more about the people in the bar. Nico and Akis, the men about our age who work at a local olive oil factory, left after their first drink, as they were heading into the main street to meet up with their girlfriends. The older couple, we learned, own the shop on the main street, the one with the postcards displayed on a stand outside. One or two more locals drift in throughout the evening, and Stelios kindly introduces us to them all, including the dog walker we saw earlier who is now joined by his wife. The villagers have all been warm and welcoming, and I feel like it's a place where we can easily become part of the community. I have a warm, contented feeling when we leave the bar and head for home.

Stelios and Eleni join us for the walk back just after eleven o'clock and when they head inside their house, Jamie asks if I'd like to grab a *gyros* at one of the cafés on the main street, the twinkling lights of which can be seen through the trees.

'I'm a bit peckish. They didn't serve any food at the village bar,' he grumbles.

'I don't suppose they have to. It's a proper bar, a place for conversation,' I remind him, realising there are hardly any pubs like that back home. 'Besides, we had dinner before we went out.'

'I know. Steak and salad doesn't really fill me up, though. Sometimes I crave fish and chips from the Codfather,' says Jamie, referring to our favourite chip shop back in Chester.

'Come on then, hollow legs.'

We head to the main street, me thinking that perhaps we should make the most of the summer months, as things will go very quiet once the tourist season ends. I don't want to be a party pooper, but we have to be mindful of income as we probably won't get any paying guests in the annexe until next year. And really we would need to generate some sort of income before then. Suddenly I'm mulling over an idea that would do exactly that ...

14

'Hi, guys!'

Three days later we are welcoming Matty and Steph to Crete. As we collect them from the airport, Steph runs towards me, bursting through arrivals with a huge smile on her face, pulling a sparkly turquoise case and wearing a dress of the same colour with a huge cream sun hat. She pulls me into a lingering hug and tells me how much she's missed me.

'I can't believe we're actually here, visiting you at your home in Greece! It still doesn't seem real,' says Steph as she links arms with me and we walk ahead, whilst Jamie and Matty, after a brief hug and some back slapping, pull a trolley with their suit-cases towards the car park, smiling and talking.

'We've just had an above ground pool installed at home,' I tell our friends as we drive. Saying the word 'home' reminds me that we really are here to stay.

'We might get a sunken one eventually, but it will do for now.'

'Oh, don't you worry, that sounds just fine. As long as you have sunloungers to chill out and sunbathe on too!'

'Naturally, it was one of the first things on the shopping list.

Although it won't all be dossing about sunbathing. There are so many places to show you around here, we want you to make the most of your time in Crete.'

'Can't wait,' says Steph, whose perfume is more noticeable in the small confines of the car.

'You smell nice, what are you wearing?' I ask.

'I couldn't tell you. I must have sprayed half a dozen samples in duty-free.' She laughs.

Driving along, Steph utters compliments about the surrounding area as we head along the beach road, before turning off for country lanes, where the landscape changes to verdant fields and rocky hills.

'It looks gorgeous here,' she comments as we drive. 'Maybe we'll fall in love with the village and buy a house here too,' says Steph.

'Ooh, I'd love that.'

I know she doesn't mean it really. Steph is a city girl who would never move away from Chester. Her holidays with Matty are usually city breaks to places like Paris or Prague, and most recently Budapest. They enjoy walking, cycling and generally keeping fit, offsetting their other love of good food.

It's almost eight in the evening when we arrive at the house, so after Matty and Steph have showered and unpacked their things, we head into the main village street for dinner at The Fig Tree.

'What a gorgeous place,' says Steph as we're sitting outside the restaurant, taking in the busy street that is alive with tourists.

We introduce Darius to our friends and he welcomes them warmly, before heading off to oversee a busy service in the restaurant this evening. Throngs of people are strolling along enjoying the warmth, and teenagers are sitting together on benches, eating pancakes purchased from a nearby stand. I observe the teenage girls giggling and flirting with the young men, watching village life unfold.

Jamie and Matty choose *kleftedes*, tasty meatballs in a rich tomato sauce, whilst Steph chooses moussaka. I have a chicken casserole that Darius told me had been simmering all day and was the speciality of the house. The food is utterly delicious and so filling that none of us can face dessert, although when a waiter places some watermelon down, Steph and I manage a juicy slice each.

As things quieten down a little, Darius returns with a tray of shot glasses and a small bottle of ouzo.

He pours us each a glass and says '*Yammas!*' as he raises a toast to us all. 'I hope you enjoy your time here in Crete.' He's looking very smart this evening in a pair of black trousers and a pale pink shirt, the sleeves casually rolled back, revealing a stylish watch on his wrist. He attracts the glances of a table of women as he walks past, and he stops to ask them if everything is okay with their meal. He works the table effortlessly, the women giggling and hanging on to his every word. It's clear he is very good at charming people. No wonder the restaurant is so popular.

'So, what do you guys' fancy doing tomorrow then?' asks Jamie as he sips his cold beer.

'Don't mind, mate, what did you have in mind?' replies Matty.

'I was thinking a bit of a hike. There's a place I've been reading about called Dead Man's Gorge.'

It's a perfect suggestion, as we all enjoy a decent walk.

'Dead Man's Gorge? That sounds a bit creepy,' says Steph, pulling a face.

'It does, but don't worry, I don't think the term applies to people who have died on the gorge,' Jamie replies. 'It gets its name because the ancient Minoans used to bury their dead in some of the caves built into the rocks, apparently.'

'It does sound a little spooky, walking amongst a burial site,' I say, agreeing with my friend.

'I wasn't exactly thinking of heading into the caves looking for skeletons, I'm not Indiana Jones,' he says with a laugh.

'Just make sure you have plenty of sun cream on,' Steph says, giving Matty, a redhead, a pointed look.

'Don't worry too much about that. There's lots of shade on the hike, apparently. And the best bit? After a couple of hours you end up on a beach with a great restaurant,' Jamie tells us.

'That's just sold it to me,' says Steph, and we all agree it sounds like a great day out.

I suggest we have a lazy beach day, the day after the hike, although a relaxing beach day to Jamie and Matty will invariably involve some type of water sport. The others agree a beach day sounds fun too.

We head to bed later and Jamie winds his arms around me.

'It's a pity the annexe isn't up and running,' he says. 'I wouldn't mind some privacy this evening.' He cuddles up close.

'You need to save your energy for tomorrow.' I plant a kiss on his lips, before pushing him away gently, when we hear laughter coming from the bedroom along the corridor.

'Sounds like someone's having fun,' says Jamie.

'Sorry!' shouts Steph. 'I was just closing the curtains and there was a goat in a tree staring right at me.'

You have *got* to be kidding me.

15

We awake early the next morning and after breakfast on the terrace, we pack our rucksacks into the car. Matty is covering himself in sun cream, stretching out his muscular arms, a result of spending his spare time lifting weights in the gym where he works as a personal trainer. The men bonded over their love of sports when they first met, particularly football.

The journey to Zakros is beautiful, driving through rugged landscape with wild, mountainous terrain and trees dwarfed by climbing cliffs rising into the distance. Wild shrubs and bushes spread along the ground, some bearing blue or white flowers. Gnarled, ancient olive trees, their huge roots spreading outwards, sit beneath a brilliant-blue sky.

'It's just so beautiful here, although I suppose the weather makes all the difference,' says Steph as we drive with the sunroof down, feeling the warm breeze on our skin, my long curly hair safely tucked inside a baseball cap.

Parking up, we head towards the entrance of the gorge. The wooden entrance sign has the words 'Dead Man's Gorge' carved into it, reminding me of something out of a cowboy film, and I almost feel we should be wearing stetsons and entering on horseback.

Jamie had said that it's less popular here than the Samaria Gorge, and there aren't too many other walkers on the trail. We tread well-defined footpaths passing clumps of wild flowers and green bushes alongside trees with yellow scorched leaves. I can feel the heat on my legs as I walk, feeling so relaxed and relishing being outside amongst nature. A bird flies overhead: its squawking feels almost eerie, breaking the near silence of the surroundings.

'You can't get a phone signal out here, can you?' asks Steph, checking her phone. 'What if we get lost? We might die and get eaten by those circling vultures,' she says dramatically.

'They're not vultures.' Jamie laughs. 'According to the leaflet I read, they'll be falcons. Although there are a few vultures and eagles in this area too.'

After an hour, we stop and sit beneath the shade of a large olive tree, take water from our bags and gulp it down.

'We'll be at that beach in under an hour,' says Jamie, lying down on a picnic rug and stretching his arms behind his head. He's developed a lovely golden tan since we've been here, which I think makes him look even more attractive. I lie down beside him for a second and snuggle into his chest.

'Oi, you two, get a room,' jokes Steph.

'I'm really looking forward to a cold beer,' says Matty, looking slightly pink. Steph roots in her rucksack, hands him some more sunscreen and tells him to reapply.

'I know I sound like his mother,' she tells me as we stroll on behind the men. 'But honestly, he's so forgetful. I've lost count of the number of times he's locked himself out of the house. He's called into my workplace on more than one occasion for my key. Good job we both work locally.'

Steph works for a high street bank.

'Have you thought of leaving a key with a neighbour?' I ask, surprised that the thought hasn't occurred to them.

'He doesn't trust them. Not since they denied all knowledge of a parcel delivery. It was in the days before the drivers took photos.'

'What was in the parcel?'

'Protein powder. I told Matty it was unlikely our eighty-four-year-old neighbour would be needing that, but he still doesn't trust him.' She laughs. 'The house on the other side has had lots of different tenants in the last twelve months, so he doesn't trust them either.'

I've also been witness to Matty's forgetfulness over the years. He's left his jacket, phone, umbrella, you name it, behind in restaurants. Though, luckily, he's always managed to retrieve them.

We walk and chat, filling each other in on recent news. I tell Steph about Milly and Sam and how she's coming out to visit in the October half term with Noah.

'That will be nice, you must miss them.'

'I do. We Skype regularly, of course, but it's not the same as being here in the flesh, is it?'

'It certainly isn't.' She smiles and links her arm through mine as we walk.

Less than an hour later, just as Jamie had predicted, we catch a glimpse of the sparkling sea in the distance, like an oasis in a barren land.

'It's not a mirage, is it?' I ask, as the rugged landscape opens out onto a pebble beach, flanked by mountains. A beach bar to the left has white tables and chairs outside, with blue umbrellas, fluttering in the breeze. We all flop down onto chairs and within a few minutes a waiter appears to take our orders.

'This is just fantastic.' We stretch our feet out, feeling the cooling sea breeze waft over us as we gulp down ice-cold beers.

We dine on a delicious meze of creamy dips of tzatziki, taramasalata and hummus, served with warm, soft pitta breads. There are plates of fried whitebait drizzled with a squeeze of fresh lemon, bowls of grilled red peppers, and salty feta cheese.

'Shall we get a taxi back?' I joke, as I stretch out beneath the sun for a few minutes, sipping a cola with ice.

'Yep. Where's the nearest taxi rank?' Steph looks around the quiet beach.

After lunch, we paddle in the crystal-clear shallow water, wishing we'd brought our swimming things, before we start the journey back.

The walk back is pleasant and leisurely, as we are all suitably refreshed, and another couple who were at the restaurant tag along with us, chatting. The woman, who is with her husband, both of them probably in their fifties, is a bit of a hoot, and keeps us entertained with stories as we walk.

'I've never been so happy in my life to see that restaurant,' she tells us. 'We got bloody lost out there, didn't we, Joe?' She turns to her husband, who nods.

'How did you get lost?' asks Jamie, trying not to laugh.

'Part of the footpath was overgrown, unless we managed to go off piste somehow. Every bloody turn was a wrong one. I had visions of us actually dying on Dead Man's Gorge.' She chuckles. 'I can laugh about it now, but it was a bit scary.'

'Don't be such a drama queen,' says her husband affectionately, rolling his eyes. 'I could see the sea in the distance, we would have found our way down eventually. Mind you, we get lost in the car with the satnav, don't we?'

'It's true.' The wife laughs. 'We ended up at the wrong church once, attending someone else's wedding, didn't we, love?' She guffaws loudly.

'Oh yeah, we did. But that wasn't our fault. Not really. What's the chances of there being two churches called St Cuthbert's within a two-mile radius?'

'I know, I remember thinking the bride had lost a lot of

weight! We'd arrived late, you see, and could only see her from the back.' They both chuckle.

'But' – her husband picks up the story – 'it was the groom who gave it away. He was at least six inches taller than the groom of the wedding we should have been at. We sloped out before they exchanged their vows, and, would you believe it, arrived just in time to hear the vows of our friends' son in the church we should have attended in the first place.'

It's a wonderful walk back to the car, as moments of silence and contemplation are punctuated with cheerful conversation as we embrace everything nature has to offer. We take shade beneath the ancient trees when we need to, sipping water and marvelling at the sight of the rust-coloured, craggy mountains that rise up towards the vivid blue sky.

'Well, it's been a real pleasure walking with you,' say the friendly couple as we all arrive back at the car park.

'You too, just make sure you have your satnav on for your journey back,' says Jamie, cheekily.

It's late afternoon when we arrive back at the house. After showering, Steph and I settle down with a book each, whilst Jamie tunes in the television to view a pre-season football match with Matty, who is admiring the tone of his skin, which has changed from a light shade of pink to a definite red.

'Have you got any fake tan?' he asks me, jokingly.

'You'd only end up orange,' says Steph, and Matty shrugs and laughs.

Later that evening we have a simple BBQ and invite Stelios and Eleni over to meet our friends. Stelios has us all in stitches with his tales and bonhomie. In the kitchen, Eleni asks me for my lemon cake recipe.

'Your friend is a wonderful baker,' Eleni tells Steph as we refresh our drinks. 'You must miss her cakes.'

'I absolutely do, but my clothes aren't quite so tight now.' She laughs. Steph would often call in after work for coffee, and would be unable to resist a slice of whatever cake was on offer to take with her for dessert.

Talk turns to DIY and Stelios tells us he is working on something very special.

'A sculpture. I love to do wood carving in my shed. I am hoping someone will appreciate it very much.'

'Ooh, that sounds intriguing. When is the big reveal?' I ask.

'Soon. I have just a few finishing touches.'

He looks very pleased with himself and I look forward to seeing the sculpture he is working on.

We wind up the evening with a Metaxa brandy from a bottle that Stelios kindly brought over, before bidding our guests goodnight and heading for bed. I'm already looking forward to spending the day with our friends at the beach tomorrow.

'You have such lovely neighbours,' says Steph as she helps me clear up in the kitchen.

'I know, they're great, aren't they? They welcomed us so warmly when we arrived here. In fact, everyone around here is super friendly.'

'So you don't really miss anything back home then?' she asks, stacking some plates into a cupboard.

'Well, you guys, of course, but Milly and Noah mainly, as I never saw an awful lot of Mum and Dad after they moved to Lancashire. Although we spoke on the phone often, I just never seemed to have the time to visit when I was running the café. I'm hoping they might come over for a holiday when it's cooler. I know Mum doesn't do very well in the sun.'

We head to bed shortly after that, looking forward to our day out tomorrow with our friends, who, despite the miles between us now, I dearly hope we will keep for a lifetime.

16

'Do you know, Elafonisi Beach is one of the most photographed beaches in Greece? It's the one you see in most of the holiday brochures for Crete,' says Jamie, sounding like a tour guide as he drives our black Fiat Punto along the dusty roads.

'I've heard it's absolutely gorgeous. I can't wait to just sit and do nothing today,' I say, relishing the thought of stretching out and sunbathing, maybe having a little swim to cool off. I've always enjoyed swimming in the sea, although it's not really something I got the chance to do too much of back in England, with the unpredictable weather, so it's another reminder of the wonderful outdoor lifestyle here. It feels like such a treat to be spending time with our friends in the sun, especially as we have both worked flat out these past few weeks, and I'm thrilled that the outbuilding is coming along nicely too with its new floor and freshly painted white walls.

Less than an hour later, we've paid for our sunbeds and settle down on the soft, almost pink sandy beach.

'Wow, just look at this water.' Steph and I have strolled into the sea having spent the last hour topping up our tans. The blue-green water beneath our feet is crystal clear and like nothing I've seen on a beach before, contrasting beautifully with the sand that has a soft pink hue, which I read is due to the thousands of broken seashells it contains. It's so unusual and stunning to look at.

Steph and I swim in the warm water, lolling on our backs and staring at the cloudless blue sky above, feeling the penetrating heat of the sun. As the salty water massages every bone in my body, I feel so fortunate and wonder how anyone could ever tire of this feeling.

As I imagined, Jamie and Matty sunbathed for all of ten minutes, Matty under his sunshade most of the time, before they strode off to see the guy at the end of the beach offering paddleboards for hire. Half an hour later, when Steph and I are back on our sunloungers reading, we spot Jamie and Matty in the water. Matty is standing confidently on his board, whilst Jamie unceremoniously falls flat into the water and I can imagine Matty laughing and ribbing him mercilessly over it.

'Ah, I'm so happy we came here,' says Steph, turning to me and touching me lightly on the arm. 'And it's not even that far really. Under four hours on a plane. It's not as though you emigrated to Australia or something.'

'Would you still come and see me if I had?'

'Of course! Although I'm not keen on spiders. Or snakes come to think of it.' She gives a shudder. Maybe now is not the time to reveal what Kostas told me about the snakes here in Crete.

'You will come back to Chester occasionally, though, won't you?' she asks hopefully.

'Of course we will! It's just nice that guests can enjoy the sunshine here on holiday. But we will come to the UK too. And we should have the annexe up and running by next spring, then I'm pretty sure I won't be able to keep family and friends away.'

'Yes, and the next time we come out, we will be paying guests. No freebies, you have a business to run,' she says firmly.

Steph knows how uncomfortable I would feel charging them, but I guess it's true, it will be a business after all.

'Okay, but mates' rates.' I wink.

I sink back into my sunbed and can feel my eyes dozing, giving myself up to the massaging effects of the sun, when I suddenly feel something wet plop onto my chest. I glance above at the sky, where a squawking bird hovers above for a second, before flying off, and I realise to my horror that I have literally been shat on from a great height.

'Aagh! Steph, grab some wet wipes from my bag.' I point furiously to my beach bag but she can barely retrieve them for laughing.

'Ugh.' I pull a load of wipes from the packet and clean myself up. 'Where did that come from?' I ask.

'It says here' – Steph is reading about the beach on her phone, when she's finally composed herself – 'that there is a bird colony over there.' She points to an islet that can be walked across to during low tide. 'There's a restaurant there too, apparently. It's a stopping point for birds migrating from Africa across the Med. You do know it's meant to be good luck if a bird poops on you,' she says in attempt to make me see the funny side.

We lie side by side and Steph asks me how we have settled into village life over here.

'It's still quite early days, but I think it's just wonderful.'

I tell her about my morning walks and how we are learning Greek, to try and integrate more with the locals. Some residents have come to recognise me on my walk now, saying good morning as I pass.

'Stelios is such a character, isn't he?' Steph smiles.

'He really is. I feel as though I've known him and Eleni forever,' I tell her. 'They are such lovely people, like chalk and cheese, although they do say opposites attract.'

'Has Jamie settled too?' she asks.

'He really has. He's even played football at a local pitch,' I tell her, although thinking about it, he only went once or twice, despite saying that the men were very welcoming after his first visit.

'That's good then. I know Matty misses him. They never stop texting each other,' she reveals, as she applies sun oil to her toned midriff. She's wearing a yellow bikini that shows off her bronzed, toned body. 'Although, I think it's mainly updates on the local football, you know what they're like.'

'Probably.' I smile, although I wasn't aware that they constantly texted each other, and wonder whether I have been a bit lacking in only contacting my own family once a week.

I glance at them out on the water. Jamie seems to have got the hang of it now, gliding easily across the sunlit sea alongside Matty. I hope Jamie doesn't miss his friend too much when it's time for them to leave.

When they eventually hand their paddleboards back and re-join us, Jamie has a huge smile on his face.

'I'll definitely have to have another go at that, it was amazing!' he says, drying himself off with a stripy beach towel.

'I might join you,' I offer.

'You should. We need to make the most of the beaches during the summer months.'

We stroll across the islet for lunch at the beach restaurant, flip-flops in hand as my feet sink into the warm pink sand. The restaurant is pretty crowded, with it being high season, but luckily we manage to find a table and dine on succulent grilled chicken with roasted potatoes flavoured with lemon and oregano.

Heading home later that afternoon, Matty and Jamie talk about their paddleboarding experience, saying they wouldn't mind trying paragliding off a mountain next and, of course, they have to mention my unfortunate experience with the bird.

We're driving along the mountain roads, feeling relaxed and happy after a really lovely day, when suddenly, as we round a bend, a car is heading towards us almost in the middle of the road and Jamie has to swerve suddenly to avoid a head-on collision. He toots his horn loudly and curses at the driver, who has already raced off into the distance.

'Bloody hell. That was close.' Jamie breathes out, looking a little shaken.

'I know! What an idiot. Are you alright?' I ask.

'Yeah, are you guys?' he turns to ask Steph and Matty in the back.

'Fine. We were really lucky there,' says Matty. exhaling.

'I told you it was good luck if a bird poops on you,' Steph comments, making us laugh and taking the tension away from the moment. Jamie drives along much slower after that, the experience having shaken him and making us feel a little vulnerable on the twisty, turny roads, only relaxing a little when we reach the wider, open ones, until we finally arrive back at the house.

17

We spend the rest of the week walking, or heading to local beaches for picnics, as well as spending our evenings in the garden having BBQs and generally loving life. Early one evening, Jamie and Matty are watching a football match, whilst Steph and I sit outside on the covered patio. I've made it a cosy space, having placed coloured lights through two huge bushes in pots. We nibble at some nuts and sip chilled Prosecco as we chat in the warm, balmy evening.

'The outbuilding is really taking shape, isn't it?' says Steph. 'Talking of shape, your builder is a fine figure of a man.' She raises an eyebrow. 'Did you say it's his brother who runs the restaurant in town?'

'Yes, Darius at The Fig Tree. I think it's the best restaurant in the village.'

'I agree, the food is amazing, no wonder it's popular. He's easy on the eye too. Even the waiters were hot.' She laughs. 'And those waitresses! No wonder young blokes hang around outside on their mopeds.'

'Yeah, Darius told me one of the waitresses is dating a local boy. Sometimes the villagers hook up with tourists too. I'm told there was a wedding here a few years ago, between a British tourist and a Greek shop owner.'

'Do you ever wish you were still single?' she teases.

'Never. Jamie is the only man for me. And one day, we really will get around to organising our wedding.'

Perhaps when the house is completely finished and our business is up and running, we can think about such things.

We're chatting away, when Kostas crosses the garden to tell me he has finished for the day. He's wearing dark shorts and a black vest that hugs his body and shows his bare tattooed arms once more.

'You've worked really late today.'

'I had no other jobs, so I wanted to work as late as possible. It's almost finished, after all.'

'Well, thank you. Would you like a beer?' I offer.

'No, thanks.' He takes a long glug of water from a bottle. 'Although that pool looks really inviting after a long day.'

'You can join us in it tomorrow if you like,' says Steph, flirtatiously, and Kostas laughs.

'Tempting, but I am heading to the beach tomorrow after work with my fiancée. She tells me I work too hard, but I say to her, how are we going to have the best wedding the village has ever seen if I don't work hard?'

He tosses his bottle into a nearby recycling bin and heads off, turning to wave as he reaches his van.

'Did you hear that? He was tempted to join us. Pity, he's such a nice man. His fiancée is one lucky woman.'

'Steph! What has got into you?' I slap her playfully on the arm. 'Is everything okay between you and Matty?'

'Gosh, I don't know, it must be the heat.' She laughs. 'Yes, we're fine. Matty is the only guy for me. No harm in appreciating good looks though.'

'Glad to hear it. Right, do you fancy going for a walk now

while it's slightly cooler? I'll show you the route I usually take in the morning.'

'Sure, why not? A walk sounds nice.'

I haven't continued with my morning walks since our friends have been here, as we sometimes have a bit of a lie-in after a night out. We're about to head off, when Stelios shouts from his garden and beckons us over.

'Ladies, I want to show you the present I have made for my wife. Tell me if you think she will like it,' he says in anticipation.

He guides us into the shed, where an object on a table is covered by a canvas sheet.

He glances outside furtively, before closing the door, and whipping the canvas away to reveal a wooden sculpture of a naked lady sitting on a rock with her feet curled under. It reminds me of the Little Mermaid statue in Copenhagen, minus the mermaid tail.

'Stelios, it's beautiful. The detail is amazing.' The figure has long tumbling hair, carved from the wood, almond-shaped eyes and a full mouth. It doesn't take me long to figure out that it's a portrait of Eleni.

'You really are very talented. I am sure your wife will love it,' says Steph.

'Love what?'

The door has been pushed open and Eleni is standing there, a puzzled look on her face. Stelios attempts to cover the sculpture, telling her she will 'ruin the surprise'.

'Stelios, what are you up to?' She narrows her eyes. 'What is beneath that canvas?'

Before Stelios has a chance to say anything, she whips the cover from the statue and her hand flies to her mouth.

'Oh my goodness, what is this?' She looks embarrassed.

'My darling, it is you. I made it for your birthday. You don't like it?' He looks crestfallen.

'Me? Then why do I have the breasts of a thirty-year-old woman?' she demands to know.

'I took it from a photograph, many years ago. The weekend we spent with friends when we went skinny-dipping. You don't remember?' A slow smile spreads along his face and Steph's eyes widen as she stifles a giggle.

Eleni ushers us both out, speaking quickly in Greek to Stelios as we leave.

'Oh my goodness!' Steph bursts out laughing as soon as they are both out of earshot.

'Hey, do you think they were swingers back in their younger years?' She nudges me. 'Going naked swimming in the sea with their friends.'

'Steph! Behave. They were probably just having fun like most young people. They were childhood sweethearts after all, are you telling me you've never been skinny-dipping?'

'Yeah, but not with other people.' She laughs again.

'Stop it! I'll never look at them in the same way again.'

Steph's eyes twinkle with mischief as we walk on.

We pass the familiar village houses, some painted white, others yellow, and one or two a pale shade of pink. Some of the residents are in their front gardens watering their plants or relaxing with a drink now that it's a little cooler, and they raise their hands and wave as we walk past. Soon enough, we are at the top of the village, near the school and the bar the locals frequent.

Back home again, sitting outside once more, I talk about the empty shop next to the supermarket where we bought the Solero ice lollies we are now eating.

'It was once a bakery!' I tell Steph.

'A bakery, huh? You're not thinking what I think you're thinking, are you?' asks Steph, turning to look me in the eye.

'What do you mean?' I reply, wondering if Steph can actually see into my very soul.

'I know that dreamy look in your eyes. It's the same look you had when you would talk about moving over here. So, spill.'

'Oh, Steph, I've had this crazy thought,' I tell her. 'We still have savings in the bank, and I'm tempted to enquire about the lease on the place. I wouldn't keep the same hours as I did back home, that's why we came here after all, but Eleni told me that people here miss the bakery. I can't stop thinking about it.'

I find myself confessing the thoughts that have been swirling around my head these past couple of weeks. 'I'm just not sure what Jamie would think about it.'

'There's only one way to find out,' she says. 'Although, a bakery suggests the locals would want to buy bread, your forte is more cakes, isn't it?' She looks a little puzzled.

'I know someone who bakes bread. She used to work at the bakery before it closed down. She's currently childminding, but I don't think it's her ideal choice of job, if I'm honest.'

'Whoa, so you already have someone lined up to work with you?'

'No, not at all. She doesn't even know I'm interested yet, besides, we've only spoken once or twice. Oh, I don't know, maybe it's a stupid idea.' I dismiss the thought as we finish our lollies.

'Maybe it's not such a crazy idea if you only opened for a few hours in the morning. I imagine you need to make an income before the annexe is up and running?'

'Yes, exactly that. Our savings would run out in no time otherwise.'

'Well, you just need to keep the work-life balance, or, as you said, it would hardly be living the dream here, would it?'

'Of course, I know, that's absolutely right.'

We head inside just as the match is finishing up and the men are discussing the merits of the England team, who have just beaten France.

'Fancy a couple of beers on the main street?' Jamie asks us as he switches off the TV.

'Why not? You're both on your holidays after all.' I smile, determined to enjoy every moment of the time our friends are here with us.

The high street is busy this evening; a coach has just dropped some visitors off in the main car park, led by a guide, seemingly heading to The Fig Tree. Darius is at the front of the restaurant to greet them, and I imagine he is pleased his restaurant is popular enough to be recommended as a stop off on a coach tour. I'm really happy his business is doing so well; he deserves it.

The tourists have probably been on a tour of the area, visiting places of local interest before stopping for an early dinner. One of the usual stops is to visit a preserved World War Two bunker off Platanias high street, not far away, which I realise I haven't got around to visiting myself yet.

'Right, guys, it's your last day tomorrow, is there anything you'd like to do before you leave?' asks Jamie.

'I wouldn't mind hiring a quad bike and exploring this side of the island, get off into the mountains,' suggests Matty.

'Great idea! Let's do it,' replies Jamie.

Heading home later that evening, we pass The Fig Tree, which has emptied out a lot now that the coach tour has departed.

'Have you enjoyed your time here in Crete?' Darius, who is standing outside the restaurant, asks Matty and Steph as we walk past and say good evening.

'It's been fabulous. And Charlie is right when she says your restaurant is the best in the village,' says Steph.

'Thank you.' He turns to me and smiles. 'I like to give a good service.'

The boys walk ahead as Steph and I lag behind, chatting.

'Oh my God, do you think Darius was flirting with you?' she asks, looping her arm through mine as we walk.

'Flirting? No, not all. Why would he do that right in front of Jamie?'

'Maybe it's my imagination then. Or the way he looked at you and said, "I'd like to give you a good service."'

'Steph! He said no such thing! Oh my goodness, you have such a filthy mind.'

Darius has been nothing but a perfect gentleman, so there is no way he would be flirting with me; I'm sure it was all in Steph's imagination. I shake my head, and go to bed smiling to myself. I'm going to miss my friend when she leaves.

18

The following day we have the most wonderful time, exploring the island on quad bikes, stopping at little beach coves for drinks. Sitting on the back seat of the bike, haring along the often-empty roads felt exhilarating, if a little scary when approaching bends, although we took them slowly after the near miss in the car. We lunched at a restaurant high in the hills, with a breathtaking view of the sparkling sea and forest below, and explored remote mountain villages off the beaten track. Steph and Matty purchased bottles of olive oil and ouzo from roadside shacks in the middle of nowhere, along with herbs for moussaka and simmering casseroles.

'That was the most incredible day,' says Matty, when we've returned in the evening. 'Just taking off like that on the bikes, not knowing where we were going. Amazing.'

'It was fantastic. I'm glad you've enjoyed your week, I hope you've seen the best the area has to offer,' says Jamie.

'It's been brilliant. I wish we were here for another week,' says Matty.

The next day as they are leaving, Steph squeezes me so hard I can barely breathe.

'See you soon, and thanks for everything. I'll miss you guys.'

Jamie hugs Matty goodbye. 'See you soon, mate,' he says, and he's a little quiet as we head home from the airport.

'That was so lovely, wasn't it? I can't wait until Noah and Milly come over in the half term. I hope the weather holds out.'

'It depends, apparently. Stelios says the weather can be a little unpredictable in October.'

'I guess, although he also said that it's been mild enough to swim in the sea in January. Can you imagine that?'

'Not really. I bet that's a strange feeling.'

Eventually, over the course of a couple of months, the outbuilding has been fully transformed, and it looks amazing.

'I think I might move in here,' I say jokingly, looking around the bright, white-walled space, which now has a modern, open-plan kitchen diner at one end. 'You've done a wonderful job. We can't thank you enough, Kostas.'

'My pleasure. And now I'm going to take a much-needed break. I will see you around.'

He smiles warmly, shaking us each by the hand, and leaves.

It's now late September and the olive man is coming to check the trees in the next week or so to see if our first batch of oil will be ready for production. Already the leaves are turning from a striking green colour to a pale shade of yellow. It's still so warm though, and we are loving being able to spend evenings outside this late in the year, something I could never do at home, and I relish spending autumn days outside in nature.

Early the next morning, I head off for my morning walk whilst Jamie snoozes. He stayed up late last night watching sport on a satellite channel and came to bed quite a while after me. I wait near the school, and soon enough I bump into Kate-rina, with the children in tow, on their way to school.

'*Kalimera.*'

'*Kalimera.* Do you have a minute?' I ask.

'Yes, of course. But first I need to get the boys into school.' She grips both of their hands tightly and steers them towards the school gates, just as a middle-aged lady in a green dress rings an old-fashioned school bell.

'Great, I'll wait here.' I take a seat on the bench.

She reappears a few minutes later with a quizzical look on her face.

'What did you want to talk to me about?' She sits next to me on the bench. Her long wavy hair is tied back today and she is wearing a denim shirt dress, looking effortlessly stylish.

I point to the phone number on the window of the empty bakery.

'I was wondering if you might help me with a phone call.'

'A telephone call?'

'Yes. Just in case there is a language barrier. I want to find out how much the rental would be on the shop.'

Katerina's eyes widen.

'You are thinking of opening the bakery again?'

'Hmm. I'm considering it. Depending on the costs, of course.'

I tell her all about the café I ran back home. When she has finished the phone call, I can hardly believe the vendor is asking for barely a peppercorn rent. Katerina tells me that the vendor thinks it would be nice for the locals to have a bakery once more.

'And if you are looking for an assistant...' Katerina smiles and I guess I was right in assuming that looking after children is not really her passion.

'As a matter of fact, I was just coming to that. Did you say you bake bread?'

'Yes. That was my job. The previous owner trained me.'

'Well, if I bake the cakes and you do the bread, then between us, maybe we could make it work. It would be back to early mornings again though,' I say, thinking of how we would need to be up by five thirty. 'Although the shop would close early in the afternoon and...' To my surprise, she suddenly throws her arms around me.

'Yes! I would love to! I am an early riser. I prefer having the late afternoon off.'

'Right. I'll be in touch,' I tell her, as we swap numbers and a tingle of excitement runs through me. Now just to tell Jamie. I feel a little nervous, but then I remember how proud he was of me for running my own café back in Chester, and I just know he's going to be happy that I'm following my passions again.

When I arrive home, Jamie is sitting outside sipping coffee from a pot he's made, staring at his phone.

'Morning, sleepyhead, are you okay?'

'Yeah, fine. I've just been talking to Matty about the football, he's going to Liverpool with a few others to watch the game against United this weekend.' He returns to his phone.

'I think they might be showing that game at one of the bars in the village. I'm sure I saw a board advertising it somewhere,' I tell him.

'Not the same as actually being there, though, is it? Or being in the pub with the other supporters.'

I'm waiting for him to smile and say, 'Oh well, never mind!' but he doesn't and I worry his words are tinged with regret.

'There are still a few tourists here, and there's always a good atmosphere in the bars when the football is being screened,' I remind him cheerfully.

'I'm not really in the mood to watch it here.' He glugs down the last of his coffee. 'It won't be the same.'

'But you've enjoyed watching the football here before,' I say, thinking he's probably just on a bit of a downer since Matty returned to England.

'It's not just the football.' He sighs. 'Nothing is really the same here, is it? I can't even make a decent bacon sandwich on a Sunday morning.'

Once more, I'm waiting for him to laugh it off, but his expression remains serious and I can feel my heart sinking.

'What's brought this on? I thought you were adapting to it all?' I say gently. 'Didn't we just have a great time, showing our friends all the wonderful things we have here in Crete? We're so lucky to be living here.'

'I know,' he says gently. 'And I've tried to settle here, I really have. But I can't lie, I still feel like I'm on an extended holiday, and that one day soon, we'll be heading home.'

'So, this doesn't feel like home to you?' I ask, disappointment running through my veins.

'Sorry, Charlie, but no.' His eyes meet mine. 'It doesn't. A holiday home maybe, but not somewhere I see myself living in the long term.'

'How long have you been feeling like this?' I ask, my heart breaking, hardly able to believe that we are having this conversation.

'A few weeks, I suppose. It was okay when I was busy working and fixing the place up, but now...' His voice trails off, before he continues. 'I barely know what to do with myself. And I miss my old friends back in Chester.'

'But we've made new friends here.'

I remind him of some of the young people we've met at the local bar, who have joined us for drinks on several occasions. I thought we were both settling in.

'They're not like our friends back home though, are they? Besides, it's easier for you.'

We're inside now and he's pacing the stone floor of the lounge.

'In what way?' I ask.

'Well, you could open a café, or a cake shop. You know, like the one in the village you're considering renting.'

'Jamie, I was only considering it.' I guiltily realise I haven't even discussed this with him yet. I ashamedly think of the phone call I had Katerina make earlier.

'Seriously considering it, by the sound of it. I heard you discussing it with Steph in the garden.'

'Oh, Jamie. I don't know what to say. I didn't mention anything right away because it was mainly just thoughts swirling around in my head. I was going to talk to you when I'd found out a little more about it.'

'And what would I do for work whilst you were running a shop? At least in Chester I had my own work too.'

'Which you hated as I recall. It's not as if I dragged you here, you agreed to it, you even booked the house viewing! Saying something about having an adventure whilst we're still young enough.'

I'm trying hard to keep my emotions in check, but I feel physically sick. I thought Jamie was fully on board with the idea but it seems I was wrong. We've made our home here, and now he's telling me he thinks it's all a mistake.

'I know, you're right, and I'm sorry,' he says softly. 'Maybe I foolishly thought I could find work in a garage here, but there are barely enough jobs for the Greek people. And I can't speak the language.'

Which is true, although we have been trying. We have been taking weekly classes online as well as practising with Stelios, who corrects us when we get something wrong. We're determined to master at least some basic phrases, but it's a difficult language and progress is slow.

When Jamie first discussed his hopes of securing a job somewhere as a mechanic, Stelios hinted it might be difficult and despite him enquiring at garages within a reasonable travelling distance, and leaving his CV, nothing has been forthcoming.

We look into each other's eyes, searchingly, and I can feel the tears welling up.

'So, what are you saying?'

My heart is thumping in my chest, dreading his answer.

'I don't know.' He hangs his head. 'My head's all over the place.'

'So you really want to head home and give up on our dream, is that it? Or maybe it was never really your dream at all,' I say, my voice breaking with emotion.

'I love Crete, you know I do, Charlie. But I realise now that it's different actually living here. I can't do it, I've tried. I'm so sorry.' Jamie buries his face in his hands.

The tears that I've been trying to hold back are falling freely down my cheeks now and Jamie takes me in his arms and brushes them away.

'Don't cry, please. Maybe we can work something out.' He sighs.

He makes us a coffee and we sit down on the sofa together, talking for what seems like forever, going around in circles but reaching no solution. In the end, we quietly accept that we want different things. I want to live here and he wants to return to Chester. It really is as simple as that. One of us would be unhappy if we had to make a compromise, which doesn't make for a solid relationship in the future.

'So you really want to go home? What will you do when you get there?' I ask, thinking of how we've sold up. I had bought the flat and café with an inheritance from my grandmother, which is now tied up in the property here. I wonder what he will do for money.

'I'll stay with my parents for a while, so I can save a little. Matty's uncle is a manager at Kwik Fit tyres and can sort me out with a job if I want one. The money isn't too bad.'

'Sounds like you've been planning this for a while,' I venture.

'Not really, maybe just the past couple of weeks. I love you, Charlie, I always will, but I can't settle here, it just doesn't feel like home to me. Would you really not consider coming back to Chester with me?' he asks, pleadingly. 'We were happy there, weren't we?' He looks at me searchingly.

And it's with this question that I realise I wasn't truly happy in Chester. I loved having my friends and family close by, of course, but I now see that I was always on the brink of burnout there. The hours I had to put into my café just to cover the extortionate rent was insane. And I would be so exhausted in the evening it was hard to really do anything but sit on the sofa. Here on the island, things feel so different. I finally have balance and sunshine and a real sense of joy in my heart that I haven't felt in years. I look up at Jamie.

'I was ready for a change.' I stand and glance out of the window at the pretty garden Stelios and Jamie have worked so hard in creating.

I feel so torn, but I really don't want to return to Chester. The life here is good for my soul and I already feel happier and healthier, as well as part of a community I am quickly growing to love. Despite my heartache, I feel as though I belong here in Crete. I know I would only regret giving all this up, which would cause resentment between us further down the line. And even though my heart breaks that Jamie doesn't feel the same way, I know my future is here. After much soul searching, we both decide there is no sense in dragging things out and Jamie says he will look for flights home as soon as possible. My heart shatters into tiny pieces.

19

After Jamie left, I spent three days in bed, only surfacing for drinks and trips to the bathroom. My appetite completely deserted me. The break-up overwhelmed me with tiredness and a need to just curl up into a ball in bed, hiding away from the world. Even when the sun streamed through my window, beckoning me outside, I still slept.

On the second day of my self-imposed isolation, Eleni knocked at the door so persistently that I flung the bedroom window open and explained that I needed to be left alone for now. She accepted my desire, but kindly left food on the doorstep, which I gratefully received and deposited into the fridge. It was thoughtful of them to look after me. Stelios had been shocked when Jamie told him of his imminent departure, saying he hoped he would return again to visit. I wonder whether he will? Maybe it's something I would hope for in the future, so that we can be friends, although maybe it would only open up old wounds. I received a message from Jamie this morning. It simply read *I'm sorry*. And I replied, *Me too*.

As I sip my coffee, I ponder the events of the last few months, wondering if I missed the signs that Jamie wasn't happy here. Or perhaps the signs were there all along and I chose to ignore them. Steph informing me that Jamie and Matty constantly texted each other proved how much he missed his friends, more than I ever realised. Thinking about it, he'd never looked happier than when they were over here staying with us recently. Despite all that's happened, I don't want any ill feeling between us. It's not as though there was anyone else involved; we just wanted different things and everyone has a right to live the life they truly want, even if it does mean making huge sacrifices.

I head outside to breathe in some fresh air when I spot Katerina walking past with the two boys, one of them running off in the opposite direction.

'*Kalimera*, Charlotte.' She lifts her arm and waves.

'Hi, Katerina.' I attempt a smile.

'Are you okay?' she asks. Maybe noting my greasy hair and pale complexion.

'Fine, I've just been a little off colour lately,' I explain.

'What colour are you today?' she asks, which, despite everything, actually makes me smile.

'Putty coloured.'

'Putty?'

'Never mind, I'll talk properly next time I see you. Right now, I think you have more pressing things to worry about.' I glance at the older boy, who is halfway up a tree.

'Alex, *ella, ella*.' She shakes her head in frustration.

He climbs down the tree with that impish grin worn by cheeky six-year-old boys. When he's down, she grips both of the boys by the hand and marches them to school, shouting goodbye over her shoulder, her tumbling black hair bouncing as she walks.

Back inside, I survey the beautiful lounge and stifle a sob. It wasn't part of my plan to be living here alone, even if I absolutely wouldn't want to live anywhere else. The sunshine makes such a difference to my well-being, and I find myself far more suited to village life. Perhaps it took moving thousands of miles away to discover the difference between Jamie and me. Maybe we weren't really the soulmates I thought we were after all, at least not deep down. Back home, our jobs took up most of our time, and the rest was taken up with friends and family, so perhaps without all of those distractions we had little in common with each other.

I take in the white walls of the room, adorned with pretty watercolours bought from the art gallery in Chania, alongside some framed family photos. There's one of Jamie and me on a beach here in Crete, arms around each other, looking carefree with the sparkling sea in the background. I recall the day clearly, me asking a woman on the beach if she wouldn't mind taking a picture. Blissful memories come rushing back.

There's a glass coffee table in front of the stone-coloured sofa with an olive wood bowl sitting on it, filled with grapes, peaches and lemons from the tree outside. I view the large, wall-mounted television. Getting it connected to the Sky Sports channels was, I now realise, Jamie's link to his life back home. Heading into the kitchen, I slide my hand over the newly installed granite worktops that complement the cream wooden units, thinking of all the hours I spent pulling up the tiles before the new floor was laid. It all looks beautiful, even though there is still a faint watermark on the ceiling that has reappeared after a fresh coat of paint and probably something that really needs checking out by a builder. Perhaps I really ought to give Kostas a call.

I pin my hair up and spend the morning cleaning up a little, before heading off to the large supermarket to purchase some flour and vanilla extract. After that, I head to a local market and buy some extra lemons and free-range eggs, as well as several baking tins from a kitchen bakeware stall that sells all manner of household items. Once I'm back home, I bake a lemon drizzle cake, chocolate brownies and some coconut raspberry buns. It feels so good to be baking again and, as I fold the flour and beat the eggs, I can feel the tension in my shoulders slowly melt away. I wondered if my cakes would taste different here somehow, but dipping my finger into the mixture I'm happy to be reminded that they taste just as delicious.

Later that afternoon, I meet Katerina outside the school and offer her and the boys a sample of my wares. The boys devour the chocolate brownies and ask if there are any more. Katerina makes appreciative noises and tells me the cakes taste divine.

'So, we're on then?' I ask, handing her my phone. In reply, she rings up the vendor and puts in an offer to accept the terms of the tenancy on the empty bakery.

'Charlie, oh my goodness, how are you?'

I had waited as long as I could to call Milly and tell her of our split. I was afraid that doing so would make it feel real, but now I had come to terms with it a little more, I knew it was time.

We talk at length about the reasons for the break-up, Jamie's difficulty settling in here, my realisation that I've never been happier. She listens with gentleness and patience.

'Do you want me to try and change the flights and come over earlier?' she asks with sisterly concern.

'No, it's fine. To be honest, I probably need to take a little time to process things. I don't want to be blubbering whilst you and Noah are here, I want you to have a great time.'

'You're absolutely sure?'

'Positive. I can't wait to see you.'

'As long as you'll be okay, that's the main thing.'

As we chat, I tell her all about my plans to reopen the village bakery. Even if I was unsure at first, in the light of what has happened between Jamie and me, I need something I can really focus on.

'So, yes, I'm pretty sure I will be okay as I have a project to think about now. Your timing is perfect for a holiday actually, before I take over the tenancy in a few weeks.'

'Oh, how exciting! I knew baking was in your blood. Are you still going to be renting out the annexe?'

'Yes, I think I am. I'm hoping it won't be too much work. Katerina has a friend who is a cleaner, so she could do the changeover cleaning, if things get busy in the shop. I'll just have to make sure I check in on the website for bookings.'

'Have you set a website up yet?' she asks.

'No, I haven't actually. Its autumn now, so I was going to leave it until next spring.'

'I could recommend a couple of sites to help you with that, if you like,' she offers. Milly is far more clued up with technology, and once even had an online clothing company selling children's things before she had Noah and didn't have the time for it any more, so I bite her hand off.

'Really? That would be brilliant!'

'And if the annexe is ready, you may get a couple of months' business in the near future, you never know. The autumn is mild and perfect for walkers and cyclists, didn't you even say so yourself?'

'That's true, but I think I'll wait to advertise after Christmas, as I want to get the bakery up and running first.'

'Good idea, but just remember how busy you were with the café back home? Make sure you strike the right work-life balance.'

'I will. I don't mind early starts, especially as the villagers like to get their bread in the morning, so I'd probably close up mid-afternoon.'

I feel so much better after chatting to my sister. She's right of course, I have to think about ways of generating money, so a website is an absolute must. For the rest of the day, I try to enjoy some late autumn sun in the garden, attempting to read my novel, although I find it hard to focus on the words. Heading inside, I think I see someone in the olive grove once more, but wonder whether it is just a trick of the light. I suddenly feel so alone. What if someone has been hanging around outside? It's been years since I've lived alone and a feeling of vulnerability suddenly engulfs me and I burst into tears.

Eventually I gather myself together, make a peppermint tea and try to collect my thoughts. I realise that now, more than ever, I need to focus on a project if I am to be happy here. I adore the open space and the weather here in Crete, and know I couldn't go back to a tiny flat in Chester. I've thought about it over and over, and although I miss Jamie, I know that's only natural after being part of a couple for so long. And it's also clear to me now that we wanted different things. I made my choice. It's up to me now to ensure I am living the best life I can.

Sitting at the table outside, lost in my own thoughts and feeling emotionally drained, I don't notice Eleni, who has quietly crossed the garden and almost makes me jump when she speaks.

'Charlotte, are you okay?' she gently asks, a frown crossing her pretty face.

She is carrying a small bottle of Metaxa brandy and two small glasses. I wipe my eyes, which I realise now were starting to tear again, and invite her to sit down. She pours us each a glass.

'I'm sorry,' I say, gratefully sipping the brandy and feeling the burn in my throat.

'Sorry for what? You have heartbreak. You are bound to be sad. But I want you to know, I am here for you.' She takes my hand in hers and I feel so happy to have made such a lovely friend. I know that living here is the right thing for me and I'm grateful to have made such good friends, otherwise I might have headed back to Chester for all the wrong reasons.

'Thank you, Eleni. I will be alright.'

We sit and chat and I reveal that I heard her crying a while ago in her garden.

'You were also sad,' I delicately venture. 'Do you mind me asking what about?'

'My friend, I suppose.' She shrugs. 'Athena was my best friend for over thirty years. We grew up together as teenagers. For a while we lost touch and then she turned up here in the village buying the next house. It was as if it was meant to be.' She takes a sip of her drink.

'What happened?' I tentatively ask.

'One evening, she went out with her husband. He likes the drink.' She mimics taking a drink to her lips.

'That evening, they visited a friend of the family in a mountain village.' She pauses for a moment and shakes her head. 'They drive home in the dark, and my friend's husband, Leo, takes a bend too fast and they crash into a tree. My friend died but he survived. They say there was drink in his blood.'

Her eyes mist over as she recounts the tale. We both sit silently for a moment.

'I'm so sorry,' I tell her, gripping her hand.

'Thank you. I am fine most days, then something will remind me. Maybe a song on the radio, or when her favourite flower comes into bloom. I just miss her. She should never have died like that.'

After a few minutes of consoling her, I try to lighten the mood by letting her in on my plans to reopen the village bakery and Eleni claps her hands together.

'What a wonderful idea! It will be most welcomed, I am sure.'

I tell her of Katerina baking the bread and trying out some of my own recipes, but something has been bothering me.

'There's only one thing,' I tell her. 'My baking is all pretty much English classics, apple tarts, sponge cakes, that sort of thing. I don't know anything about making baklava or Greek desserts.'

'I can teach you how to make the baklava,' she says, sounding more excited than I've heard her in a long time. 'And there is a Greek walnut cake that you must include too. It's called *karidopita*. No flour in the recipe, only breadcrumbs. Drizzled with a honey glaze, it is delicious.'

'Oh, that does sound good.'

My stomach gives a little rumble, and I realise it's the first time I've felt hungry in days.

When Eleni leaves, I take one of her recently delivered pies from the fridge and cut a generous slice, eating it in front of the television. Flicking channels, a romantic movie is about to start and I switch over immediately, unable to cope with that right now, instead settling on a repeat of *The Great British Bake Off*, which might even give me some inspiration. After the show, a football match comes on. I think of Jamie and a silent tear rolls down my cheek. For the umpteenth time, I wonder how I didn't sense how unsettled he was, although he obviously hid it well. I suddenly feel a deep sense of hurt that he never tried to talk to me about it until it was too late.

But as I sink my teeth into the delicious cheese pie, a shaft of sunlight beams through the window, warming my spot on the fabric sofa. And, despite my situation, I manage a smile. Something tells me that I'm going to be alright.

20

I'm clearing up in the kitchen the next morning when the phone rings. It's Steph, who is heartbroken for me.

'Oh, Charlie, are you okay? I've been ringing you.'

I'd had half a dozen missed calls and texts from Steph when I'd retired to my bed for a few days after Jamie's departure. I'd replied to her first text but couldn't quite bring myself to talk just yet.

'I know. Sorry, Steph, I slept a lot. I was going to call you today actually.'

'Oh, Charlie, I had no idea Jamie was thinking of coming back to England, I hope you know that.'

'I know, thanks, don't worry.'

'I guess it explains all those phone calls and texts though,' she says with a sigh. 'To be honest, I had a bit of a go at Matty for not saying anything, but he swears he didn't know Jamie was that close to coming home. He said he thought he was just homesick and the feeling would soon pass.'

'I'll be alright, Steph, don't worry about me. It was my decision to stay here, which, despite what's happened, I don't regret.'

We chat for a while longer and I tell her all about my plans for the bakery and that she's welcome to come over for a girlie weekend whenever she likes.

'Try stopping me! Especially if your cakes are on the menu too. Listen, if you want a chat any time, day or night, you know I'm here for you, don't you?'

'Of course I do, thanks, Steph.'

After doing a few jobs around the house, I head out for a walk, a little later than usual. Taking my usual route, I walk past The Fig Tree, which is a little quiet today as the season begins to wind down. Darius is sitting at a table drinking a coffee and talking to Stelios. I wave and attempt to walk on, but, of course, Stelios beckons me over. I look a complete mess, with my hair pinned up and bags under my eyes. I wish I'd taken a different route.

'Charlotte, please join us.' Stelios wraps me in a hug and Darius looks a little awkward, but beckons a waiter to bring me some coffee.

'I am sad that Jamie has left,' says Darius, a little unsure of what to say next. 'I hope you are okay? Perhaps you would like a little brandy in your coffee?'

'Thanks, but it's a little early in the day for me,' I say, not wanting to go down that road.

'Of course. Well, if there is anything you need...'

'Thanks, Darius,' I say, once again appreciating people's kindness.

He excuses himself and heads off into the kitchen, as Stelios takes my hand in his.

'If there is anything Eleni or I can do, please let us know. You are part of our village now,' he says warmly.

'Thank you, Stelios, for everything. I don't know what I would do without you both.'

'Tonight, you must come to dinner with Eleni and me. Meet

my son, Apollo, who is home for a few days from university. Maybe you bring some of your lemon cake.' He winks.

I'm in no mood to socialise and try to explain this to Stelios, but he refuses to take no for an answer.

'I realise you are sad, but being alone will only make you feel worse. Seven thirty,' he tells me firmly.

I finish my coffee and head off, eventually finding myself standing in front of the empty bakery, staring at it. I imagine a pretty sign displaying the words *Charlotte's Bakery*, in feathery gold strokes against a pink background. I picture the counter inside displaying delicious cakes and treats and I feel a smile spread across my face. Later that afternoon, I lie in the sun outside feeling the heat of the rays on my skin and dare to feel a little bit optimistic about my future. I made my choice and I want to live here. In fact, right now there is really nowhere else I would rather be.

Back in my kitchen, I bake the lemon cake as requested by Stelios, set it out on the side to cool, and then settle down on a sunlounger outside again. Closing my eyes for a minute as the sun appears from behind a cloud, I think maybe I'll just have ten minutes...

I awake with a start, realising it's almost six o'clock, which means I've been asleep for over an hour and a half. My mouth feels dry and my head feels a little sore. I'm also shocked to discover that my straw hat from the top of my head has disappeared.

Getting to my feet, I'm about to head upstairs for a shower, when I spot the errant mountain goat from the corner of my eye, chewing on my favourite straw hat. Give me strength!

21

Apollo is a younger version of Stelios, handsome and slim, and just as animated as his father. He regales us with stories of university life, over some snacks and a glass of ouzo, whilst the meat sizzles on the BBQ. After a few minutes, I'm surprised when Darius appears at the door, carrying a large raspberry cheesecake that Eleni gratefully receives.

'*Kalispera.*' He's looking smart but casual, in a pale-yellow polo shirt and long black cotton shorts. He shakes Apollo warmly by the hand before embracing him.

'So how does it feel to be home, after being in Heraklion?' Darius asks him.

'I like it.' Apollo takes a sip of his beer. 'The city can be a little crazy at times, but I like the nightlife. You're only young once.' He raises his beer and says '*Yammas*' and we all raise our glasses.

'I hope it is not all partying,' Stelios teases. 'I am looking forward to the day when I can introduce my son as a doctor,' he states proudly. 'You must take your studies seriously.'

'Of course I do, Papa. Work hard, play hard. Didn't you teach me that yourself?' he replies and Stelios laughs.

We dine on succulent marinated lamb and chicken, slices of grilled halloumi, and flatbreads. I have little appetite, but, despite myself, I enjoy the evening as the company is so engaging, distracting me from my thoughts. When the night winds up and we have said our goodbyes, Darius escorts me to my door.

'Thank you, Darius. No doubt I'll see you around.'

'It is my pleasure. If there is ever anything I can help you with, please say,' he offers sincerely.

'Thanks, I appreciate that. Goodnight.'

'*Kalynichta.*'

Back inside the house, it feels empty and silent. I suddenly feel so alone and the reality of my situation hits me once more. I head to bed with a lump in my throat that quickly turns to tears and I curl into a ball and cry myself to sleep.

Early the next morning, I'm in the kitchen sipping orange juice after a restless sleep, when I hear the rumble of a truck pulling up outside.

Heading out to the front, I see that it is Manos, who has some machinery on the back of his truck.

'*Kalimera.* This morning I come to take your olives,' he informs me with a smile.

In truth, I had completely forgotten the date he told me he would be coming, and vow to start writing everything down in a book, or at least buying a calendar to circle dates on, like I did back home.

'Of course.' I lead the way and soon enough he is in the olive grove. The gentle drone of the machine that shakes the olives into nets fills the air as I watch from a distance, hardly able to believe that he is actually harvesting olives from my very own olive grove. Despite my heartache, I feel a sudden sense of pride. This house, this land, all of it belongs to me and the realisation shocks me a little. I take a deep breath and inhale the scent of the warm pungent earth arousing my senses as I walk beside the trees behind the harvesting machine. An hour and a half later, Manos is ready to leave having finished his work.

'Thank you. I will be leaving now. I will be in touch when your bottles of olive oil are ready. Your olives should make around twelve bottles, maybe more.' He smiles warmly and departs. I realise I know nothing about the production process. I must ask Darius if he would like some for his restaurant and maybe offer some to Stelios too. But today I have some other business, as I'm meeting Katerina and together we are going into town to sign the lease on the shop.

Waiting for her outside the school, I can't help wondering whether Jamie would have been on board with the idea of me running the shop, and, if he wasn't, would I have abandoned any thoughts I had harboured? I recall the conversation we had before he left. He seemed down about the idea of me running the bakery. So maybe I wouldn't have gone ahead with things if Jamie was unable to find work of his own. He wasn't keen on working in the bakery with me, that I know. But then, surely he realised we needed an income before the annexe was taking guests next year?

I'm starting to think that perhaps there is a reason things worked out the way they did, when my thoughts are interrupted by the sound of Katerina calling my name.

'Good morning, Charlotte. How are you today?' Her enthusiasm is infectious.

'I'm fine, especially now that I'm doing something about my future here as a single woman.' I sigh.

She opens her mouth in shock and I tell her all about my split with Jamie as we drive into Chania.

'I can hardly believe it. Are you sure you are okay?'

'Don't worry, I'll be fine. I'm excited about the bakery, and it will certainly take my mind off my love life, so maybe it's come at a perfect time.'

'I'm off men for life.' She pouts. 'I was with a guy for two years, before he ran off with someone else.'

'Well, he must be crazy,' I say and I mean it. Kat is beautiful and kind and is fast becoming a good friend.

'Thank you. I'm over it now, it was a year ago.' She shrugs and it makes me wonder how long it will take me to get over Jamie.

We head inside the letting agent's, stepping onto the marble floor. A ceiling fan whirrs overhead and the coolness washes over us. It's unusually warm for October, the sun still hot, especially around midday. A short while later, I've signed the lease and I'm handed the keys to the bakery. We head outside into the warm sunshine once more.

'Right, I think this calls for a celebration before we head back,' I say excitedly, waving the keys in the air. We head into a local restaurant for an early lunch and toast our future with a glass of champagne.

After lunch, Kat tells me about a clothes store down a side street that has the most beautiful dresses at great prices. I'm not really in the mood for a shopping spree, but it's good to know of such places and I thank her for showing me around. She purchases a cool white dress, a patterned dress in swirly autumn colours and some vest tops.

'I like to wear vests under my apron in the bakery when I'm baking the bread. The oven gets so hot,' she explains.

'Aprons! Good idea. Do you know a shop where we could buy some? Actually, I think I'll order some online with the name and logo.'

'That's a great idea,' agrees Katerina.

Early that same evening, having successfully ordered some aprons, we meet at the bakery and scrub it from top to bottom, until even the bread oven shines. A little after nine thirty we head into the village bar for some well-deserved refreshments. It's quite busy this evening and so Kat takes it as an opportunity to do some impromptu advertising. She proceeds to tell everyone about the bakery, and a ripple of excited chatter can be heard throughout the bar.

'About time, too,' says an elderly man in a flat cap, raising his glass. 'The bread in that supermarket, it almost takes my teeth out.' The other customers laugh and I realise that this could be something that the village really needs.

Kat and I walk along home together, and I discover her family home is only a ten-minute walk away from mine. It's a yellow-painted house with a large front garden. She tells me she lives with her parents and two younger brothers and dreams of moving out and getting her own place one day. I say goodnight and take my leave.

On my way home, I pass by The Fig Tree restaurant. The evening is winding down and Darius is standing outside alone smoking a cigarette.

'Kalispera,' he greets me. 'How are you today?'

'I'm okay actually. I've had a really busy day. We've been preparing the bakery. I've taken over the lease. It opens next month.'

'That sounds exciting. I'm sure the locals will look forward to it opening. Me included.'

'Thanks, Darius. Actually, I meant to ask you something earlier. Would you like some olive oil for the restaurant?'

'But of course, as long as the oil is good,' he tells me honestly. 'My father used to harvest olives and make his own but he sold off some of his land. Why do you ask?'

I tell him all about Manos taking my olives to produce some oil.

'There isn't a huge amount but he seems to think the olives are of pretty good quality,' I tell him. 'I'm going to have around twelve bottles, which I'll never use on my own.' The words 'on my own' stick in my throat. 'So I would like to give you some.'

'Then I would be more than happy to accept, thank you.'

'You're welcome. Well, goodnight then.'

'*Kalinichta* Charlotte.'

Before I turn to leave, Darius opens his mouth as if to say something else, but suddenly changes his mind. I continue on my walk home, wondering what it could have been.

It's been a busy day and after all the cleaning at the bakery earlier, and a couple of beers at the bar, I feel exhausted. For the first time in a while, I climb into bed and I'm fast asleep as soon as my head hits the pillow.

22

I turn the key in the car engine but nothing happens apart from a pathetic squeak. Damn! I'm collecting Milly and Noah from the airport this morning. It's a little after nine thirty and I knock at the home of Stelios and Eleni, but their car isn't in the driveway so it looks like they've gone out for the day. Milly and Noah will still be airborne right now, so I guess I'll just have to take a taxi to the airport to meet them.

Heading towards the local taxi rank, I run into Kostas, who is just leaving a café in the village centre. He looks handsome even in a dust-covered black vest, grey shorts and battered work boots.

'Kostas, hi! How are you?'

'I am well. I've just finished a job here in the village and now I'm heading home. Are you okay?'

I tell him all about my car failing to start, the irony not lost on me that Jamie is a mechanic and probably could have fixed the problem in no time at all.

'I'm just heading to a taxi rank. I'm meant to be collecting my sister from the airport,' I explain.

'I will take you,' he says decisively.

'Oh no, I couldn't possibly ask you to do that.'

'You didn't ask. I offered.' He smiles.

Five minutes later we are sitting inside his blue car and I'm relieved it isn't his work van. I could just imagine Milly's face if I turned up at the airport in that. It will already be a shock, I'm sure, that I have a man in tow.

'I hope you don't have to be somewhere,' I tell him guiltily as we drive along. 'I wouldn't want to ruin your day.'

'I have nowhere to be.' He shrugs. 'I would probably drink too much beer in a bar somewhere with a couple of friends, so maybe you are saving me from myself.' He turns to me and grins.

I'm wondering why he isn't spending the day with his fiancée, but decide it's none of my business.

Driving along the coast road towards the airport, I think of all the times Jamie and I took this journey, from our very first holiday to the viewing trip to the house. The excitement we felt stepping off the plane, the evenings sitting in restaurants beneath the stars gazing out to sea. I swallow down a lump in my throat, the memories too painful to recall.

'So, your sister is coming to stay with you? That will be nice,' says Kostas, pulling me from my thoughts.

'Yes, she's bringing my six-year-old nephew, Noah, too. I can hardly wait to see him, he's such a lovely little boy.'

'Luckily, the weather forecast is pretty good this week, maybe twenty-two degrees, which is probably warm enough to swim in your pool. Warmer than England, I imagine.'

'Oh, that is good news as I was hoping it might be mild. Noah will love the pool. And that is definitely warmer than home, the central heating would be on and warm coats dug out by now,' I tell him.

'It is a little cool for me, but I imagine for someone British it is okay.' He laughs.

'That's so true.' I giggle.

We pass the time pleasantly and I notice Kostas hasn't asked where Jamie is today, although maybe Darius has told him all about the situation. Then again, I'm not sure why I would be a topic of conversation between them.

'Thank you, Kostas,' I tell him when he drops me off at the airport. 'You've been more than kind. We'll take a taxi back to the village. I'm not sure how long they will be collecting their baggage.'

'I will wait here. You have no need for a taxi,' he insists firmly.

'Well, if you really insist, then thank you,' I tell him. To my surprise, he parks up and joins me inside the airport. I imagine Noah wondering who this man is, here to greet him and his mother.

Half an hour later, Milly is trundling her suitcase through arrivals alongside Noah, who is pulling his little blue Trunki case. His face lights up as soon as he spots me.

'Auntie Charlie.' He runs towards me and flings his arms around me.

'Hiya, Noah, how are you?' I kiss the top of his head, smelling the gorgeous scent of children's shampoo, before I give my sister a lingering hug.

'This is my friend Kostas, who kindly gave me a lift to the airport today.'

Milly shakes hands with Kostas, who takes her case like a gentleman.

On the way to the car, I tell Milly all about my own car conking out as I was supposed to be collecting her.

'Good job you had a knight in shining armour who came to your rescue,' she whispers.

'I know. Very lucky. He did the work on the outbuilding too.'

'Skilled *and* kind, eh?' she says, eyeing him up as he walks in front, Noah beside him with the little case, asking him questions.

'Are you checking him out?' I ask in mock horror.

'As if.' She laughs.

'Wait until you see his brother.' To my shock, the words come tumbling out of my mouth. Milly stands still for a second and stares at me.

'Oh, my word, it didn't take you long to eye up the local talent, how long has Jamie been gone? A few weeks?'

'Don't be ridiculous, I'm just saying, he looks like his brother, Darius, who runs a local restaurant, although I think Darius is even better looking.'

'Do you now?' Her eyes widen.

'Stop it, I'm just saying! Men are obviously the last thing on my mind, my heart is breaking inside, what are you like?' I slap her on the arm playfully.

'I know, I'm sorry, I'm just teasing you. Really, how are you doing?' She takes my hand and gives it a little squeeze.

'I'll be alright, just a bit shell-shocked at the minute, that's all. But I'm so thrilled you're here!'

Twenty minutes later, Kostas has deposited us outside the house. I wave him off gratefully after he refuses the offer of petrol money. Noah has run ahead into the garden, looking around at everything and asking when he can go into the pool. Maybe I'm already acclimatised, as I'm not sure it's hot enough for swimming, but Milly tells me it feels really warm and the weather is gorgeous.

We head inside and after a cool drink and a snack, we change into our swimming things. Noah is kitted out with Spider-Man armbands and a shark swimming ring I bought especially. We all jump into the pool and start swimming around, throwing a ball and having fun.

'So how are things going with Fireman Sam?' I ask.

'I wish you'd stop calling him that,' says Milly.

'Sorry, I will.'

'All good, I think.'

'You think?'

'Yeah, he's great, we have a lot in common and we have fun together.'

'But?'

'Oh, I don't know. He's been to my house and we go out a lot, but I've never really been to his place. He said it needs doing up and is a bit of a building site, but... Oh, never mind, I'm sure it's nothing,' she says, painting a smile on her face.

I can't help thinking that if it was nothing, it wouldn't be bothering my sister, but I get the feeling the conversation is over, for now at least.

It's late afternoon, so we decide to go for an early dinner later, and plan a day out for Noah tomorrow. Perhaps we will go into Chania and take a ride in a glass-bottomed boat. Noah loves boats and, thinking about it, it's not something I've done since I've been here.

We have pizza later at The Fig Tree and Noah's eyes light up at the sight of a strawberry sundae. I introduce my sister to Darius and, when he leaves our table, she turns to me.

'I see what you mean, he *is* good looking. What's his story? Is he single?' she asks, checking he's out of earshot.

'He seems to be. I think the restaurant takes up most of his time,' I say, thinking of how much time he seems to spend here.

Just after eight thirty, Noah is yawning so loudly that it's clear it's time to head back to the house. As I pay the bill, I ask Darius if he has any recommendations of where to take a child on a day out.

'Maybe a trip on the little train that runs through the village? It heads off into the hills and on to various places. One of the routes takes you through Thalassa Gorge, the only gorge you can actually drive through. You pass lots of mountain goats on the way, he might like that.'

I've seen the little white train on the high street, giving a toot toot of its horn as it passes through the village on its way back to Platanias main street, where the booking office is.

'That actually sounds like a really good idea, thanks, Darius.'

I had imagined Jamie taking Noah on little bike rides, or mucking about with him in the pool, and feel almost guilty that he has no male to bond with, either here or at home.

Darius bids us goodnight, before he disappears with one of the waitresses, a pretty woman in her twenties with long dark hair, and I find my eyes following them as they climb into his car.

Back home, Milly and I sit outside beneath the stars, sipping a glass of wine whilst Noah is safely tucked up in bed. She tells me she's only recently introduced Sam to Noah as a 'friend'. But says she gets the impression he isn't that keen on children.

'Which is hugely disappointing, if I'm honest,' she says as she sips her wine. 'I mean, don't get me wrong, I'm not looking for a substitute father for Noah or anything, but sometimes I get the impression he would rather it was just us two.'

'Well, that's no good, you come as a package.' I can see how Milly might have strong concerns.

'Exactly. I suggested a day out to a theme park last week, the three of us, and something came up at the last minute, which meant he couldn't go. Although I notice he never cancels when Pixie's babysitting for the evening.' She sighs.

'Would I be right in thinking you have a few serious reservations about the relationship?'

'Truthfully? I think I have. This holiday may give me the opportunity to really think things through,' she says, smiling. 'I can't even think about a long-term relationship with someone who doesn't bond with Noah. He will always be my priority.'

An hour later, we're both pooped so we head inside for an early night. Milly and Noah are staying in the house with me, although she's already looked at the annexe and declared it fabulous. I'm determined to make sure both Milly and Noah have a wonderful time here before I think about the bakery. And the beginning of a new life without Jamie.

23

We're seated on the little white train, Noah jumping up and down excitedly as the driver toots the horn, and off we go. We're lucky to have the carriage to ourselves as there are only ten of us on the train today.

'Where are we going?' asks Noah as we trundle along, taking in the sights, passing shops and restaurants until soon enough we turn out of the main street and over a bridge, spying tall grasses and reeds poking out from the riverbank.

'We're heading to the Grand Canyon,' I tell him, which although it sounds very grand, in reality is just another gorge.

Driving along, the scent of wild garlic and rosemary wafts in the warm air, reaching our nostrils and I delight in the sight of the beautiful flora and fauna. Trees in various shades of green rub shoulders with wild bushes and plants and the occasional burst of a red wild flower.

Along the mountain road, the train slows down and, just as Darius had predicted, several goats with bells around their necks make their way towards us.

'Look, Mummy,' Noah cries excitedly to Milly, as a brown

goat with a black beard raises his head, sniffing inside the carriage.

'He's after your Pringles.' I laugh as Noah tentatively offers one to the goat, who quickly gobbles it down. Soon enough, three more goats emerge from the bushes, bells tinkling, looking for titbits. Noah throws a few crisps onto the floor, the goats jostle for them and the driver toots the horn as we drive on.

The road ascends, and we disembark at a pretty village at the top of the gorge. It has a small high street with a handful of tavernas, a gift shop and a stall in the car park selling jars of raki, honey, and olive oil soaps.

After a delicious lunch of chicken *gyros* and freshly squeezed orange juice, we take a little look around a war museum that has the shell of an army tank outside the entrance.

Noah asks if he can climb up and I take a photo of him in the seat of the rusty tank. A young museum worker, standing outside on her phone taking a break, comes over and shows Noah how the gun moves up and down by winding a handle. It's a little stiff, but Noah soon manages it.

'I've got a gun at home,' he tells the young woman, who looks a little surprised.

'A Nerf gun,' Milly explains. 'A toy with foam bullets. They're all the rage with young boys.' She rolls her eyes and the young woman laughs.

'Yeah. I got some new bullets last week, didn't I, Mummy? A packet of fifty. Uncle Jamie said he will make a target for me to shoot at in the garden.'

Milly and I exchange a glance as my heart pains for Noah, the innocent casualty in our break-up.

'Right, that's enough gun talk. How about we go and pick some nice juicy oranges?' I ask Noah as the next part of the journey involves heading to an orange grove and picking your own fruit. Milly chats to Noah about the fruit and talks of maybe getting a juicer when they get back to the UK for freshly squeezed drinks each morning, although, in reality, I'm not sure how she will have time for that before the school run.

'Plenty of vitamin C for those winter mornings,' I tell her, feeling happy that hopefully I won't have to suffer colds and flu and freezing winter mornings in my new home.

When we climb back onto the train, Noah has eight large juicy oranges in a hessian bag and a jar of marmalade, purchased from the little farm shop at the olive grove. We stop and take photos of the magnificent gorge below before we trundle off onto the mountain road once more.

When we disembark from the train three hours later, we all agree that it's been a lovely day out.

'Can I have an ice cream, please?' asks Noah, as we pass a stand outside a shop on the main street, displaying a rainbow of different colours and flavours.

'Let me get these,' I tell Milly, as she's about to retrieve her purse from her handbag.

Milly and I both choose pistachio flavour and Noah licks his chocolate ice cream as we stroll back to the house, Noah already asking if he can go in the swimming pool.

It's a fine day for October, the sun still high in a clear blue sky, so I tell him yes, and that I will join him for a game of ball in the pool shortly.

Darius is chatting to a staff member and strolls to the entrance of the restaurant when he spots us walking past.

'*Kalispera*. Did you enjoy your afternoon?' He walks towards us, smiling.

'Oh, we really did, thanks for the recommendation, Darius.'

'Noah enjoyed it too. It was beautiful, and a relief not to have to drive around those bendy roads,' adds Milly.

'And a goat ate some of my Pringles,' Noah tells Darius, which makes the man smile.

'Well, I am happy you are enjoying your time here. Maybe you should come and have a strawberry sundae at the restaurant before you leave. On the house!' He directs his comment at Noah.

'Does that include me?' asks Milly cheekily.

'No. Children only. I have to make a profit.' He laughs, before heading off.

'He really is lovely, isn't he?' Milly says with a sigh, watching Darius, who is wearing a white T-shirt and black shorts, sunglasses pushed on the top of his head.

'I suppose he is a nice man.' I shrug, appreciating his qualities, but men are the last thing on my mind at the moment.

We spend the next few days visiting local beaches and relaxing. Playing crazy golf on the main street in Platanias was a particular highlight for Noah, who was surprisingly good, considering his age. Stelios also invited us to a BBQ one evening and he kept Noah entertained with a series of card tricks that had my nephew wide-eyed in amazement.

Thankfully, the car didn't have a big problem and I collected it from a local garage the day after Kostas kindly took us to the airport. I'm so relieved there wasn't a major issue with the car, as I didn't want to have to rely on any more goodwill from my new friends and neighbours, despite their insistence that they are happy to help. The sense of community is something I really love here: I barely had the time to say little more than good morning to my neighbours in Chester, as we were all so busy dashing around. But the people in this village seem only too happy to rally around and help each other out, which is truly humbling and heart-warming.

'When are you coming home?' asks Noah, hugging me tightly as we say goodbye at the airport, and I can feel a lump forming in my throat.

'Greece is my home now, remember? But I'll be over soon to see you and your mum.'

'Do you promise?'

'I promise. I couldn't stay away from you for too long.' I squeeze him tightly.

My heart is twisting as I drive home, already missing them both, and not for the first time I wonder if I've done the right thing in staying out here alone. Then I get a grip and tell myself most people probably feel this way when they say goodbye to loved ones. I have to do what makes me happy, more so than ever now that I am on my own.

Back home, I idly flick on my lettings website. I had contacted the company Milly had recommended and they had set me up with my own page before I knew it! As the site loads, I'm stunned to find an enquiry about a booking in March next year. It's from a bloke who likes to walk, and has been researching the area. I send an email and a few minutes later, the booking is complete. It seems I will have a new guest staying in the spring, and who knows? It might be the beginning of lots of guests making regular bookings. Suddenly it all feels real and I'm excited, and maybe a little scared, all at the same time.

The next morning, I awake early with a stiff neck having slept strangely last night. I had a weird dream where I got lost in Dead Man's Gorge and was eventually airlifted to safety by a helicopter and flown over the mountains to hospital. As I grab my robe and head downstairs, I can hear the faint sound of dripping water and wonder if I have left a tap on. Walking into the kitchen, I gasp as I see water dripping through the ceiling in the kitchen.

I'm about to go across and see if Stelios can help, when the ceiling suddenly crashes open and I'm covered in a deluge of water, my screams filling the early morning air. When it's over, the plaster surrounding the hole dangles down forlornly either side of the kitchen light fitting.

I dash upstairs to dress and by the time I return downstairs Stelios is banging on the kitchen door, joined by Apollo, both of them looking concerned.

'We heard the screams. What on earth has happened?' asks Stelios, already heading inside.

I guide them into the kitchen to show them the damage and, unable to contain myself, I burst into tears.

'I knew I should have had that watermark on the ceiling checked out,' I sniffle, as Apollo roots in the cupboard and locates a bottle of Metaxa, handing me a small glass.

'It's eight o'clock in the morning,' I remind him, as Stelios hands me a tissue.

'It's for the shock. You can have a shock at any time of the day.'

'Eleni and I will clear up here. Apollo, take Charlotte out for breakfast,' Stelios instructs his son.

'No, really there's no need,' I protest, but Apollo is already on his feet, as Eleni appears at the door wondering what's happening. Taking in the scene, she dashes to find a mop and bucket from the cupboard under the stairs. I protest once more as she begins clearing up, but realise I am shaking and maybe I do need to get a little food inside of me.

We head to a little café on the main street, and Apollo orders coffees and some pancakes. I down a strong, rich coffee that really hits the spot, but pick at the pancakes, drizzled with honey and blueberries, that Apollo eyes up after he has finished his own.

'Help yourself.' I push my plate towards him and he devours my second untouched pancake. Apollo has the most exceptional smile and a shock of curly black hair that makes him look really cute and I imagine there are no shortage of girls interested in him at university, especially as he has a kind, laid-back personality too.

'Thanks for this, Apollo. I seem to be making a habit of inconveniencing people this week.'

'I have nowhere to be,' he says with a shrug. 'I'm taking some time out and relaxing.'

'Well even so, I really appreciate it. Your parents have also shown me nothing but kindness, I can see where you get it from.'

Feeling calmer after the coffee and a chat with Apollo about university life, we head back, chatting easily as we walk. As we round a corner, I throw my head back and laugh at something Apollo tells me, as Darius walks out of the newsagent's.

'*Kalimera*. Are you okay?'

His eyes flick from me to Apollo and back again.

'Yes, fine. Just having a coffee whilst Stelios assesses some damage in my kitchen.'

I tell him all about the leaky roof and how Stelios will be in touch with Kostas to see if he can repair it.

'Kostas is on holiday.' He looks thoughtful for a minute. 'You know, things are a little quiet in the restaurant now as the season is winding down.' He looks at his watch. 'Give me an hour and I will see what I can do.'

'You?' I say in surprise.

'Yes. I know some of Kostas's friends in the building trade, so I can get some supplies and fix the ceiling. Will you be at home all day?'

'I have no choice, there's a hole in my ceiling. I really could have done with it in the stifling summer heat, cheaper than running the air conditioning.' I manage to muster a smile.

By the time I return, all the water has been mopped from the kitchen floor and the plaster consigned to an outside bin.

'Thank you so much,' I tell Stelios and Eleni. Stelios is fretting over who to contact, having learned Kostas is on holiday.

'Don't worry, Darius is calling over later,' I reassure him, explaining the situation.

'Oh, right. Good, good. If he needs any help, he must shout me.'

Eleni whispers something in his ear.

'Of course.' He slaps his forehead. 'I forget. We have to go to the big supermarket this morning to shop. Is there anything else we can do before we leave?'

'Nothing at all. You have been more than helpful, thank you.'

Apollo is on his phone, replying to a text that has just pinged through.

'I would offer to help too, but my friend in Agia Marina has just asked me if I want to go out sea fishing.'

'You've all done enough,' I insist. 'Now go and enjoy your day.' I thank them once more for their kindness.

The ceiling caving in is the last thing I need, as exactly one week today the bakery will be opening its doors and there's still so much to do. The signwriter is arriving tomorrow to erect the sign above the bakery, and I ought to be feeling excited now, yet I just feel overcome with emotion and sheer exhaustion. I'm hoping that baking and doing what I love will revitalise me.

I'm washing some bedding after Milly and Noah's visit, when I hear a tap on the door. It's Darius.

'There will be some plasterboard arriving in one hour,' he tells me. 'I will be back then; in the meantime, I will go and retrieve my tools. Are you okay now?' he asks.

'Yes, fine. It's just the last thing I needed to happen right now, but hey, worse things have happened.'

Like being left by your fiancé while you start a new life in a foreign country, for example.

'Okay, please send me a message when the plaster arrives.'

'Shall I phone the restaurant?'

'I will put my number in your phone,' he says, taking my

mobile from the coffee table and tapping his number in, which I'm not sure whether I find too assertive or not.

'Oh, right, thank you.'

'And, please, if there's anything apart from the ceiling that I can help with, please let me know.'

When Darius leaves, I sit down on the sofa, as a shaft of sunlight filters through the window. I curl up with a cushion behind my head, and my eyelids feel suddenly heavy. I can feel myself drifting off...

Suddenly I wake up to the sound of banging on the door. After a man has unloaded a sheet of plasterboard from his van, I quickly text Darius to tell him that it's been delivered. Thank goodness the kitchen doesn't have the traditional beams in the ceiling, as there are in the lounge, or it might have been a huge, expensive job.

Darius arrives shortly after, wearing cargo pants, a fleece and carrying a toolbox.

He gives a little shiver as he steps inside.

'Are you cold?' I ask in surprise.

'A little. It is only around eighteen degrees today.'

'Only? It still feels quite warm to me, although I think the log burner will be going on in the next few weeks,' I tell him as we walk through to the kitchen. 'Thanks for this, Darius, I didn't realise you were a builder too,' I say as he sets up some tools, having been to retrieve a ladder outside. He's so easy to talk to that I find myself enjoying spending time in his company, more and more.

'I'm not a builder exactly. Just skills I have learned from my father,' he tells me.

'And you're a chef too! Obviously good with your hands,' I say, before realising what that sounds like.

'I've had no complaints,' he says with that cheeky grin. 'About my cooking, I mean. Although these days I prefer to manage the restaurant and leave the cooking to a chef I have trained.'

He retrieves a tool from his box that locates any wires in the ceiling. 'Right, I think I should get on with this before the light fades.'

'Of course, I'll make some coffee,' I say, heading to the kitchen, feeling grateful that Darius is here to help. I also find myself wondering whether there is anything going on between him and the waitress from the restaurant...

24

Darius tells me he can patch up the ceiling, but Kostas will need to check the lights when he's back as the water had dripped down through the fittings.

'He will be home in two days' time, if you can manage without the kitchen light until then. He is the only one of us who is a qualified electrician.'

'Where has he gone on holiday?' I ask, firing up the coffee machine.

'Just a short break to Heraklion to visit some old friends. Maybe to get over his heartbreak,' he reveals, going on to tell me that his fiancée called time on their engagement. 'They were together for three years, but truthfully? I'm not sure she was right for my brother.'

'Why not?'

'I don't know. She complained he worked too hard, yet complained that he never spent enough money on her, also. It would appear he could never please her.'

Chatting as he works, Darius tells me a little more about the skills that he and Kostas learned from their late father, but also tells me that his heart was never really in the building trade.

'I always preferred cooking and dreamed of one day opening my own restaurant.'

'So, you're living the dream then?'

'I like to think so,' he says, continuing to saw the plasterboard. 'It can be hard work in the summer months, but I love what I do.'

Over the next hour, Darius saws and measures, heading up the ladder to fit the new ceiling. Then he checks the position of the ceiling, reaching up high and revealing a taut, tanned stomach as his T-shirt rides up. I find myself averting my eyes.

'Right, that should be okay.' He finishes up and places his tools away in his toolbox.

'Thank you so much, Darius, would you prefer cash for the work or can I transfer some money into your bank account?'

'Please, there is no need. The materials cost hardly anything, trade price from a place Kostas uses. And my time I was happy to offer whilst the restaurant is quiet.'

'I couldn't possibly allow you to do this for free. At least let me take you for dinner to say thank you.'

He pauses for a moment, and I wonder whether I have said the wrong thing, or if he might have got the wrong impression, thinking my intentions are not entirely neighbourly, when nothing could be further from the truth.

'Or maybe not. I'd feel better if I could pay you, though,' I quickly add.

'No payment, I insist. It was nothing. If you would like to take me to dinner, then thank you, I will be happy to accept. Although my restaurant is the best in the village,' he says, jokingly. 'So I am not sure where you will take me.'

'Maybe somewhere in another village then. I'll drive.'

And if I'm honest, I feel more comfortable with that, as I don't want tongues wagging around here about my private life.

'Okay. Well, I must head back to the restaurant as I have a

few jobs to do. I will be back in a couple of days to plaster over the board.'

He heads off and I walk out into the rear garden, when once again I see a figure in the olive grove. This time when I head closer, the figure remains. I'm about to turn on my heel to see if Stelios is home when the man steps closer.

'Please.' He raises his hands. 'Don't be afraid, I mean no harm.'

The man, who looks to be in his sixties, is wearing a dark blazer with a pale-blue shirt underneath and a pair of beige chinos. He has a slightly unkempt grey beard and a bald head with grey hair at the temples.

'I just wanted to see the house,' he explains.

'What do you mean, see the house? Have you been hanging around here before?'

'Once or twice. I am sorry if I scared you,' he says gently. 'This house,' he continues, 'was once my home.'

I suddenly realise this must be the husband of Eleni's deceased friend.

'Oh, I see.'

'My name is Leo. I left the house not long after the accident.' He removes his cap and runs his fingers through his thin hair.

'I just wanted to see who had bought it, and how it looks now. Sorry for being so secretive, but people in the village, they blame me for the accident. I will leave now.' He places his cap on his head, and turns to go.

'Without even taking a look inside?' I find the question tumbling out of my mouth. My heart truly goes out to him. Whatever the circumstances, he is still a husband mourning the death of his wife, after all.

His eyes light up as he follows me inside. Taking in the décor, his eyes mist over a little.

'It is beautiful, you have done a very nice job. I hope you will be very happy here.'

I introduce myself as I make us some tea. I'm surprised that the house had stood empty for so long, but Leo explains that he couldn't bring himself to sell it at first. As we sip our tea and enjoy a slice of lemon cake each, he tells me that after the death of his wife he went to live with his brother in a village called Maleme, a couple of miles away. 'He is also a widower, so we keep each other company,' he explains. 'I miss my friends here, especially Stelios. But I know Eleni, and others, blame me for the death of her friend.' He shakes his head regretfully as he sips his tea. 'I tried to explain the truth about that evening, but she would never listen.'

'The truth?'

'Yes. We had been across the mountains to visit a relative of my wife who lives in another village,' he explains. 'I have small glass or two of wine with some food, but I was not drunk.' He pauses as he recalls the evening. 'As we drive home, my wife is feeling a little... how would you say?... giddy from drinking the ouzo.' He speaks slowly and carefully, his English not as good as Stelios's. 'She asks for radio on,' he continues. 'She turns the dial, swaying and singing loudly when she finds the music. When we approached a bend, without warning, she...' He pauses.

'Are you alright?' I ask gently, as he struggles to go on.

'Yes, yes.' He takes a sip of his drink and composes himself. 'She grab steering wheel, she say animal is in road.' He pauses again. 'I lost control of car and we crash into tree. She hit her head.' He stops talking again for a moment and takes a deep breath. 'Two days later she die. The police, they breathalyse me and all everyone hears is that I took too much of the drink. I know that I was not drunk but my test did show I was just at the limit.'

'But how would anyone know that?' I ask.

'Someone in village has a grandson who is an officer of the police. These things always get around.'

'Did you ever tell anyone the true story?' My heart breaks for him as I listen to the sad tale.

He shakes his head. 'I do not want to blacken the memory of my dead wife,' he says loyally. 'I stayed friends with Stelios for a little while,' he continues. 'He came to see me at my brother's house. He was kind. But Eleni will never forgive me. Things can never be the way they once were.' There is a faraway look in his eyes as he speaks.

'Oh, Leo, I'm so sorry.'

'I have taken up enough of your time. Thank you for your hospitality. *Efcharisto*.' Leo stands to leave just as there is a knock at the front door. I'm surprised that Darius is returning so soon, but when I open the door with Leo at my shoulder, Eleni is standing there in front of me. Her eyes widen in surprise when she sees my guest.

'What are you doing here?' she asks, her gaze flicking between us both.

'Please go and get Stelios,' I say gently. 'I think a heart-to-heart between you three is long overdue.'

I arrive at the restaurant just as Darius is about to leave and I tell him about the situation at the house.

'Leo is back? That's a surprise.'

'He told me a few things about what happened on the night of the accident with his wife. Things that people maybe aren't aware of,' I reveal.

'Really?'

'Yes, I'm sure you will find out in time but I'm not sure it's my place to say anything just yet.'

'Of course.' He holds his hands up. 'Is he alright?'

'I think so, yes. I've left them alone to have a talk, hoping they can resolve a few things. It must have been so hard for him leaving the village when he was still grieving.'

'I hope they manage to sort things out, I really do. Friends in the village can be a lifeline.'

I sit and have a drink while I wait. I wanted to give the three friends some space to talk, hoping they manage to resolve things between them. It seems so sad that a lack of communication has caused all of this uncertainty, although I guess that is often the cause of relationship breakdowns. It saddens me that the three friends lost each other at a time they probably needed each other the most.

Half an hour later, I return home and the three of them are still in the garden. Eleni is red-eyed from crying, twisting a handkerchief over and over in her hands. Stelios and Leo look as if they have been crying too.

They beckon me over as I approach the house. Leo stands, shakes my hand and thanks me.

'Forgiveness is something we all need. If we are ever to have any peace in our life,' says Stelios. 'We are only human after all.'

'Welcome back to the village,' says Eleni quietly and the weight lifted from Leo's shoulders is almost visible.

25

Darius returned late last night, after the friends had departed, to retrieve something he had left behind and stayed for a brandy afterwards. Later, we both reached for the door handle at the same time, and I felt something pulsate through my veins as our hands briefly touched. I closed the door behind him, confused, and tried to put it out of my mind.

However, I have other things to focus on, as it's full steam ahead for the opening of the bakery tomorrow. I feel an excitement in the pit of my stomach. Hopefully, things will be busy, so before Leo heads home – he ended up staying with Stelios and Eleni last night – I go over to my neighbours' house and tentatively ask him if he would consider doing a little gardening for me.

'Are you serious?' He looks slightly shocked by the suggestion.

'Absolutely. Just some grass cutting and general pruning. Maybe every two weeks? Perhaps the odd bit of maintenance too, should the need arise.'

For a second, I feel guilty not asking Stelios as he has worked so hard on the garden, but then again, I think he was being charitable when we first arrived, as he hasn't offered to do any work since.

'I would like nothing more. It would be nice to have a link to the house, thank you, thank you.' He grasps my hand, tears filling his eyes.

'I'm being entirely selfish,' I tell him, not wanting him to think I am offering him work out of charity. 'I'll be doing a lot of baking and hopefully the shop will get busy. I don't want the garden to suffer, we have worked so hard on it.'

'I can see that,' he says. 'I love this garden. I regret it was so neglected when you purchased the house.'

I spend the afternoon baking at the shop, feeling slightly nervous, hoping my cakes will be well received by the locals. I'm waiting for Katerina to arrive shortly, so she can sample the walnut cake and give me her honest opinion of it.

Half an hour later, she arrives breathlessly at the bakery, just as a van pulls up with supplies.

Standing outside, I take in the sign that has been erected at the front of the shop. The signwriter has done such a good job; the words *Charlotte's Bakery* gleam in fine gold lettering against a pink façade. I feel such a sense of pride looking at it. My own bakery, here in the heart of a Greek village.

'*Kalimera*, Charlotte,' says Katerina brightly. 'How are you? I think I might burst with excitement,' she says, letting out a little squeal.

'I'm excited too, but a little nervous, I must admit. What if people have become accustomed to buying their bread at the supermarket? And maybe they prefer the taste of baklava to my cakes.'

'Pah, don't be silly. People love freshly baked bread in the morning. And your English cakes! I am sure they won't be able to get enough of them,' she reassures me kindly and I can only hope that she's right.

I invite Katerina to try the *karidopita* walnut cake that Eleni taught me. It's still warm and has been drizzled with honey.

'Oh, this is delicious!' She wipes her mouth with a paper napkin as honey dribbles down her chin. 'It tastes just like the one my grandmother used to make. I'm sure this will be a big hit.'

'I hope you're right.' I think of the Greeks who have probably been making these cakes for most of their life.

As well as the squares of walnut cake, I have carrot cake, chocolate brownies, lemon drizzle and a huge Victoria sponge. Katerina has also made several trays of baklava with pistachios.

'Right, see you bright and early in the morning,' says Katerina at a little after seven o'clock as we lock up.

Strolling home, we pass Apollo seated outside the village bar with two friends. He beckons us over to join them for a drink.

'I have to be somewhere,' says Kat, glancing at her watch. 'And don't be staying out too late,' she tells me jokingly, pointing at her watch as she departs.

'I won't. Maybe just one drink. It might help me to sleep.' I laugh.

I join Apollo and his two friends for a beer and he wishes me well with the opening of the bakery tomorrow.

'My mother is beyond excited. She is crazy for your cake.'

'That's good to hear, I hope other people will be too,' I tell him. 'Not forgetting Katerina's bread, of course, which is very tasty.'

'So is she,' mutters Ralf, one of Apollo's handsome friends.

'Really? Well, I'll be expecting you to be a regular visitor to the shop,' I tease and he tells me he doesn't think that Katerina would even notice him, as she is so beautiful. I'm surprised he is so unsure of himself. He seems like an engaging and very handsome young man.

After thanking Apollo for the drink, I head off, leaving the boys to their evening ahead. They tell me there is live music at a bar in the village later and it's a shame I have to go to bed early.

As I stroll along, my thoughts suddenly turn to Jamie and I find myself wondering what he's up to in Chester. I've kept myself so busy these last couple of weeks in a clear attempt to block him from my thoughts, but I wonder whether things will catch up with me one day, suddenly leaving me an emotional mess. And what was that tingling feeling I felt when Darius and I both reached for the door handle last night? For now, I think it's time to put all of my energy into my new venture and not risk any more heartache.

I barely sleep for excitement, and the next morning, I wake as my alarm rings out at five thirty.

Glugging down a coffee, I take the short walk to the shop as dawn is breaking, with the promise of a nice day ahead. Birds are singing and I inhale deeply, enjoying the dawn chorus, truly happy to be here, even if it is on my own. The trees are changing colour, yet are still a pale shade of yellow, as opposed to the rich russets and reds of the autumn trees back in England.

Katerina is already outside when I arrive at the shop, and jumps up and down when she sees me.

'I thought you'd be inside,' I say in surprise, as she has a set of keys too.

'Not on the first morning. It is your shop. You should enter first.'

I hurriedly unlock the door and we step inside. I feel a tingle of pride looking at the smart interior. We're opening up at eight o'clock, and I have my fingers crossed that there may be a queue of expectant customers when we open the doors.

An hour later, the shop is rich with the smell of baking bread, as I set the cakes under plastic domes and the traybakes on plastic trays. I quickly whip up some blueberry scones and some plain shortbread, so the counter is soon filled with all manner of tasty treats.

'Gosh, I feel sick,' I say to Katerina as I rearrange the shortbread and some chocolate chip cookies for the umpteenth time. 'What if hardly anyone turns up? I'm not sure what I'll do with all of this cake.'

'Relax,' she says, taking a load of farmhouse loaves from the oven before placing a batch of baguettes and rolls in to bake.

With a few seconds to eight o'clock, I place some free samples on the counter, before casting a final glance around the shop. I head to the door to find three people outside, two of whom are Stelios and Eleni, brandishing a bottle of champagne, ready for the grand opening. I've hung a string of bunting outside in pastel colours and put a poster in the window advertising the baked goods inside.

'Congratulations!' They step inside and Stelios's eyes light up as he notices the samples of bread and cakes on the counter.

I thought about having an official opening at lunchtime, but Katerina assured me that the morning would be a great time to start, as the shop is close to the school and parents would call in after dropping their children off. My stomach twists in knots, when over the next hour a constant stream of customers pop into the shop, mainly to buy bread, but observing the rows of cakes on the counter and sampling some, buying other things too. It's all going far better than I even dared to dream. An elderly lady in black speaks to Katerina in Greek before pointing to the walnut cake. She takes a paper plate and offers the old lady a slice. The grey-haired lady nods as she eats.

'Good,' she declares, buying several pieces as well as two baguettes and a lemon drizzle tin loaf. I can feel my heart soar; getting an endorsement from an elderly Greek woman is such a compliment. Throughout the morning, customers curiously taste the cakes before buying, and by lunchtime almost everything has sold out, leaving only a few loaves and rolls in baskets, along with a handful of scones and rather a lot of Victoria sponge, which doesn't seem to have proved quite so popular.

'Wow, what a successful morning! I'd say that went well.'

'How could it not?' says Kat confidently. 'We make a great team.'

Katerina and I toast the morning's success with a glass of champagne, clinking our glasses together as a customer walks into the shop. It's Darius.

'*Kalimera*. I see you have had a successful morning.' He glances at the almost empty trays underneath the glass counter. 'I must offer my congratulations; you are the talk of the village!'

'Really?' I say in surprise.

'Yes. I have been in three shops this morning and at each place I hear women standing around talking about your cake.'

'Is there anything I can tempt you with?' I ask, as Katerina takes some trays to a sink to wash.

'Are we still talking about the cakes?' He raises an eyebrow, and I, annoyingly, find myself blushing.

'Err, yes, very much so.'

He smiles. 'I came to wish you well. And maybe buy some of your English sponge.' He gestures to the Victoria sponge under the glass dome. 'Two slices, please.'

'Are you just feeling sorry for me because I have some cake left over?'

'Of course not. Well, maybe.' He grins.

I place the cake slices into a small cardboard box and, finding a nearby piece of ribbon, tie a red bow around it.

'Thank you.' Darius smiles. 'My guest will appreciate that.'

Just after two o'clock, we finish cleaning: the place is gleaming and ready to lock up for the day. It's been a busy morning. I will spend some time at home baking this afternoon, then I have lots of time to relax. It feels so different, having the rest of the day off, especially compared to the long hours I kept at the café back in Chester.

Saying goodbye to Katerina, I head off home, thinking I might take a little siesta before I do the baking for tomorrow. It's been a successful day and I'm so grateful for that. But as I'm leaving I do find myself wondering who Darius's special guest is. Who would appreciate the ribbon around the box? Could it be the dark-haired waitress from the restaurant?

26

It's a mild evening, so at around seven o'clock, I take a walk before my planned early night – I need to be ready for opening in the morning, after all. Making my way along the main village street, I notice there are hardly any diners in the restaurants, as the season winds down.

Turning down a side street, I find myself heading towards the beach, lured by the sound of the crashing waves. I pass hotels and apartments, many with their pools covered, and sunloungers stacked up and protected in tarpaulin. Passing the Scandinavian bar, my heart sinks as I recall the evening Jamie and I spent there. It's hard to believe that things could have changed so quickly after that.

I feel the wind through my hair as I walk, passing a young woman, and an elderly man walking his dog. In the distance, boats are moored up and there's a kiosk selling tickets advertising special prices for the last of the season's boat trips.

There's a bar with several diners seated at a terrace, so I decide to stop for a coffee. A young man serves me quickly, and I order an omelette, not feeling like cooking for myself this evening. As I stare out at the wild, untamed sea, the waves crashing onto the beach, I reflect on how much my life has changed these past few months. I know, deep in my bones, that I love it here. Even in late October, it's mild enough to just have a cardigan thrown over a pair of cropped trousers and a T-shirt. And I adore the relaxed pace of life and real sense of community here.

Finishing my tasty omelette, topped with crumbly feta, I'm about to leave when I hear a voice.

'Fancy meeting you here.' It's Kostas, dressed in shorts, a vest and running shoes.

'Kostas, hi, what are you doing here?'

'Running.' He places his hands on his knees and breathes deeply. 'I realised I am not as fit as I thought I was, so I have started to run along the beach again.' He glances at his phone. 'Eight kilometres. That is enough for one day, I think. May I join you?'

He orders a Greek coffee and a fruity, herbal tea for me.

'I hear your opening day was a success,' he tells me as he sips his coffee.

'It really was. I hope it wasn't just curiosity. I have this fear that no one will turn up tomorrow.'

'I don't think you have anything to worry about. The village has missed having a bakery,' he reassures me.

'How's things with you? Are you busy with work?'

'Surprisingly so, and I am very grateful. Since I split with my fiancée, it has kept my mind off things.'

'What are we like, hey? Two lost souls.'

'Let's drink to that.'

We clink our cups together.

'In fact, let's have a proper drink,' says Kostas. 'I need to get home and shower, but I'll buy you a drink at the village bar if you fancy it, shall we say an hour from now?'

Maybe he's just being friendly, but I certainly don't want him to get the wrong idea. I hesitate for a moment. But then think, it's just a friendly drink, surely it can't do any harm? After all, neither of us are looking for a new relationship so soon – both recently heartbroken – and I need all the friends I can get right now.

'Sure, why not? That will be nice.'

He drains his coffee and stands. 'I'll run back – burn off a few more calories to allow for the beer.' He winks, and then he's gone.

After showering at home, I dress in a pair of jeans and a white shirt, pairing it with a black necklace. I then head off towards the bar just off the high street, where Kostas is already waiting. He looks attractive in a pink short-sleeved shirt and blue jeans. When he greets me with a kiss on both cheeks, I notice how good he smells. He heads to the bar and a few minutes later we're both sipping cold beers and picking at some nuts from a bowl.

'So, tell me what happened between you and your fiancée. That is, if you don't mind me asking.'

'Of course I don't mind.' He takes a sip of his beer. 'Maybe she was right, perhaps I did work too hard. I don't think we spent as much time together as we should have, for a couple who were engaged to be married,' he muses.

'But weren't you saving for the best village wedding of all time?' I remind him. He considers this for a moment before he answers.

'I told myself so,' he tells me honestly. 'But maybe, deep down, I was putting it off, always wanting to save a little more.'

'Perhaps. It's strange how our inner thoughts control our actions, isn't it?'

'Yes, you're right, it is.' He nods, thoughtfully. 'Maybe I should have been more honest with her, no wonder she thinks I'm a pig.' He shrugs and takes a sip of his beer. 'And what about you?' he asks.

'Well, to be honest, I thought everything was fine, which I

realise probably sounds a little stupid.' I sigh. 'But Jamie simply couldn't settle here. I suppose he loved me, but he loved his old life back in England more,' I tell him truthfully.

'Being in a relationship is overrated anyway,' says Kostas. 'And being single means I can sit in a bar having a beer with whoever I want.' He raises his glass. 'Here's to being single.'

'You have a point.' I raise my glass too, although I'm not quite feeling the joy of being single just yet...

We have a couple more drinks, chatting easily: me talking about the bakery and him telling me about a job he is working on in a nearby village, pulling down an old extension and replacing it.

'It wasn't the most pleasant of jobs, I found a rat and a snake. Two snakes actually.'

'Did you have to mention the snakes again?' I pull a face.

'I've told you: they are harmless enough. They do have toxins, but they are not deadly in humans,' he tries to reassure me.

A little after ten o'clock, I find myself yawning, and make my excuses to leave.

'I have to be up early. Thanks for suggesting having a drink, I've really enjoyed myself this evening, Kostas. It's good to spend time with people, it makes you think less about your own problems.'

'I agree, you can never have too many friends. Goodnight, Charlotte.'

We stand outside the bar and he wraps me in a friendly but lingering hug, just as Darius walks past.

'Brother! Would you like to have a drink with me?' Kostas asks him good-naturedly when he notices him.

'Of course. I closed the restaurant early, as it was very quiet this evening. Can I tempt you to another?' he asks me.

'I'd love to, but I have an early start tomorrow. Another time though. I still owe you a meal, remember.'

'I'll hold you to that.' He meets my gaze, his dark eyes illuminated by a street light, and for a second I'm almost tempted to risk the exhaustion in the morning and stay out for a while longer.

As I take the short walk home, I can feel his eyes following me. It's a feeling that surprises and confuses me at the same time.

27

'So, what do you think?'

Darius has dipped some bread into a bottle of the olive oil made from my very own olives. He chews it thoughtfully, before abandoning the bread and grabbing a teaspoon and sipping it directly from the spoon.

'I really like it. It has quite a peppery finish, which is good. How many bottles do you have?'

'Only twelve.'

'I will take them all from you. But I will pay.'

'There's no need. I wanted to give them to you, especially after you did the work on the ceiling. Although, I kind of remember saying I would take you out for dinner.'

'Which I haven't forgotten,' he tells me.

'I haven't either. It's just that I've had a lot on lately.'

'Then maybe you could let me know when you have nothing on.' He smiles that cheeky, boyish smile once more, and I will myself not to blush again.

'Maybe Sunday? Lunch somewhere?' I suggest.

The village shops are closed on Sundays, observing a strict tradition that Sunday should be a day of rest, restaurants only opening for a few hours in the middle of the day for lunch, especially now that the tourist season is all but over.

'Okay. I'll look forward to it. Maybe we could take a walk around the Botanical Gardens,' he suggests. 'It isn't far from here and the restaurant there is in a very pretty setting.'

'A day out walking amongst nature sounds really nice actually. A chance to recharge the batteries.'

I start to head off just as my phone rings with a video from home. It's Milly. Noah is proudly showing me another of his Lego creations; this time it's a space station.

'I'm going to be an astronaut when I grow up,' he tells me.

'Are you now? Like Buzz Aldrin.'

He looks at me, a little confused. 'Don't you mean Buzz Lightyear, Auntie Charlie?'

'Yes, silly me. Although Buzz Aldrin went to the moon first. Ask your mum to show you some YouTube videos.'

'Thanks, sis, that's me doing nothing else for the evening. He's currently obsessed with space.'

'Oops, sorry.'

'Actually,' says Milly, who's dressed in a stylish burgundy-coloured jumper and a grey scarf casually draped round her neck. 'I'm ringing to ask if you've thought about what you are doing for Christmas. Are you coming home? I don't like to think of you there all alone at that time of the year.'

I'm wondering why she's mentioning Christmas when I realise it's almost November. It's still so mild here that it's easy to forget exactly what time of year it is.

'Christmas? Gosh, I honestly haven't given it a thought, although I suppose the months are racing by.'

I've been so busy with the house and the shop, yet Milly is right. Everyone is with their family at Christmas time, aren't they?'

'Most of the flights from the islands will have finished by

then,' I explain. 'It might involve a costly flight to Athens first, but I'll definitely have a think about it.'

'Well, we'd love you to be here. Mum and Dad are coming over too.'

'And Sam?' I ask.

When Noah runs off to play, she speaks softly into the screen. 'No Sam. We're done. I'll call you later and fill you in.'

The news doesn't come as too much of a surprise, given Milly's concerns whilst she was here.

I head to the shop and bake some of the cakes for the following day, returning home a little after nine o'clock. I pour a glass of wine and call Milly back, who tells me all about Sam and how her instincts about him not being comfortable around children were true. They'd had a conversation one evening, about whether Noah would be an only child and he'd told her that he could never see himself having kids. Apparently they weren't 'on his radar'. They split shortly afterwards.

I finish the call with my head filled with thoughts of Christmas, wondering how things will be here and whether I ought to be at home in the bosom of my family instead. I know my friends, especially Stelios and Eleni, will make me as comfortable and welcome over the Christmas period as possible, and Katerina, who has become a good friend, will almost certainly feel like going on a night out or two. Apollo may be home again for Christmas, and even Kostas has become a friend to me now. And then there's Darius. The only man who has stirred even a vague feeling of something in me, which I don't even want to remotely acknowledge, as it would be foolish to embark on anything new so soon after Jamie. Besides, apart from a little teasing, he hasn't given any hint that he finds me remotely attractive.

All these thoughts swim through my head and tiredness soon takes over. As I snuggle down to sleep, exhausted after a busy and productive day, I pull the cosy feather duvet around me, moulding my body into its soft layers. I smile to myself, glancing at the silvery moon outside through a chink in the curtains. I look forward to another jam-packed day in the shop tomorrow, and thank my lucky stars.

Over the next two days, the bakery is busy with customers, and I dare to hope that it's been a great success. I'm beginning to know the regular customers, and I've been able to practise my Greek with Katerina so that I can chat with them a little. Today, many customers have bought a selection of cakes in boxes for after Sunday lunch tomorrow, knowing the bakery will be closed. It feels wonderful to know I have a whole day off, and I'm already looking forward to spending some time just relaxing and heading out to a new restaurant.

'So where is Darius taking you tomorrow then?' Katerina is sipping some peach tea as we take a short break during a lull in sales, turning the sign to closed.

'The Botanical Gardens, I think. He said something about it having a nice restaurant.'

'Oh, it's absolutely lovely there, you feel like you're in a jungle, surrounded by gorgeous palm trees and colourful flowers. Make sure you wear some flat shoes,' she advises.

Glancing at the front door, I notice a young man hovering outside.

'Looks like a customer, I'll open up.' I drain my tea and head to the door. When I open it, I recognise the young man as Ralf, Apollo's friend from the bar.

'Hi.' I smile brightly. 'How are you?'

'Good, thanks. You?'

I can smell his citrusy aftershave, which, if I'm honest, he may have gone a little overboard with. He's dressed in smart jeans and a tight-fitting grey T-shirt that hugs his muscular body.

He heads to the counter and chats to Katerina in Greek, his voice sounding surprisingly nervous.

'As if you eat bread,' she says in English, maybe not wanting to exclude me from the conversation. Her eyes rest on his toned body and Ralf is temporarily rendered speechless.

'Er, for my mother,' he stumbles, his confidence from a minute ago seeming to have deserted him.

'Well, baguettes are popular, and most people like my big buns.' She points to a basket of large bread rolls.

'Ooh, yes, your buns do look very tasty.' Poor Ralf has completely lost his cool.

'Maybe a tin loaf?' I suggest, wading in, lifting one from a basket and placing it into a bag. He thanks me but then loiters for a second. I make myself scarce in the back, wondering if he is going to ask Katerina out. But, to my surprise, he suddenly turns on his heel and dashes out of the shop.

'Poor Ralf, were you playing with him?' I ask Katerina as another customer leaves with some cakes.

'What are you talking about?' She looks at me in genuine surprise.

'You weren't flirting? I saw you check out his flat stomach, when you made the comment about him not eating bread.'

'No, I was just stating a fact. Gosh, do you think he thought I was flirting?' She suddenly looks mortified.

'Would that be so bad?'

'Yes! I would never chase a man! Especially one who is so good looking,' she says, with a dreamy look in her eyes.

'Are you kidding? He thinks that about you too.'

'He does? But Ralf could have his pick of anyone. Besides, how do you know that?' she asks.

I tell her about the comment in the bar and she puts her hands on her cheeks.

'Oh my goodness, really?' She seems completely shocked.

'He'll be back, I'm sure of it. He's bound to want to take a look at your big buns.' She looks completely mortified and I can't help but burst out laughing.

Looking at pretty Katerina, her tumbling black curls tied back in a band and delicate heart-shaped face, I'm surprised she thinks that Ralf wouldn't give her a second glance.

'What are you doing this evening?' I ask Katerina as we lock up later that afternoon.

'I'm going to the cinema in Chania with a couple of friends I made when I did the school run with the boys,' she tells me. 'Would you like to join us? There will be English subtitles.'

'That's kind of you, but I'm a little tired. Maybe next time. Although the next time you go and watch a movie, it might be with Ralf.' I wink.

It's a pleasant day, the sun still warm as I walk home. I peel off my cardigan and feel the heat of the sun on my arms as I walk. I pass Eleni, sitting outside her house under the porch with two of her village friends, chatting and drinking tea. One of the women raises her arms and waves.

'Wonderful cakes!' She points to a plateful on the table in front of her, purchased from the bakery. Eleni beckons me over.

'Thank you, I'm pleased to hear it.'

'Sit down, have some tea,' she offers and I politely decline.

'Thank you, Eleni, but I must get on. I need to take a shower, and I have some paperwork to do.'

When I arrive back at the house, Leo is in the garden working. There is a pile of pale yellow and brown leaves that have been raked into a mound in the middle of the lawn.

'*Kalispera*, Charlotte. I will just get rid of these leaves then I will be on my way,' he says cheerfully. Looking at his face, the stress and worry seem to have been mostly erased, and as he stands here in the late autumn sunshine, he looks younger than he did when I first encountered him that day in the olive grove.

'Thank you, the garden is looking good.'

As I imagined, Leo has actually been a godsend, the garden being something I don't need to think about, instead giving all my attention to the bakery. Any branches have been neatly trimmed, the lawn mowed and my flowers in pots carefully pruned.

I ask him what his plans are for the rest of the day and he tells me he is having dinner with Stelios and Eleni later, before heading to the local bar where he will have a game of dominoes with Stelios and some old friends. Leo revealed that his village friends had never really turned their back on him, but his own survivor's guilt had kept him away from the village. I'm so happy things have worked out for him. He tells me he is happy living with his brother, so has no plans for a permanent move back here, but is pleased he can visit and reclaim a part of his old life in the village.

It's Saturday evening, so after I've given the house a quick clean, I shower then settle in front of the television with a glass of wine. I'm just wondering about what to make for dinner, not really feeling like cooking, when there's a knock on the door. Eleni offers a bowl of home-made moussaka.

'I have made far too much,' she tells me. 'And I don't have much appetite. I think maybe I should not have had that second piece of cake.'

'Eleni, you are a lifesaver. I was just stressing about what to have for dinner!'

I tuck into the tasty moussaka and pour myself another glass of red wine, before flicking on the television. I watch a pop quiz, followed by an episode of *Midsomer Murders*, and by ten o'clock I'm barely able to keep my eyes open, so I head upstairs to bed. As I drift off I find myself really looking forward to my day out tomorrow with Darius. Sunday really is a day of rest.

28

I wake to a shaft of sunlight streaming through the windows the following morning, just before eight o'clock. Grabbing my robe, I head downstairs and fling the doors open, as a warm breeze filters into the kitchen. It's another glorious day!

'Oh, you're back then, are you?'

The goat is standing on top of the outbuilding again.

'Where have you been these past weeks? Although when I have paying guests in there, you'd better stay away,' I tell it, as it cocks its head to one side. 'I mean it. I don't want them being spooked. You'll have to make do with the trees, if you insist on climbing.'

It opens its mouth and makes a loud braying sound in reply.

'Good. I'm glad we understand each other.'

'Who on earth are you talking too?'

I swing round to find Darius standing at the garden gate grinning. I pull my robe tightly around me.

'Darius! What? Oh, never mind, just the goat.'

'I realise I forgot to tell you what time we would leave today and as I was on my way back to the restaurant, I thought it would be easier to swing by. Would ten thirty be okay? It's around a thirty-minute drive away. I just have a few jobs to do in the restaurant first.'

'Perfect. The weather seems lovely too. Though it's probably global warming,' I mutter, half to myself.

Darius smiles. 'Or that Crete is the most southerly of the Greek islands. It can often be like summer in late October, even November. Sometimes not so good, but today, we are lucky.' He smiles. 'Oh and wear some flat shoes, the landscape is a little up and down,' he tells me, just as Katerina did.

'Okay. I'll meet you at your restaurant.'

I grab some orange juice from the fridge and a little Greek yoghurt and honey, before changing into a pair of white cotton cropped pants and a pink vest top. I grab a cardigan from a hook in the hall in case it turns chilly later, although looking at the blue skies I'm hoping that won't be the case. I pull on a pair of white trainers that have a few sparkly bits on and pile my curly hair on top of my head with a clip. A slick of lip gloss, and I'm ready to go.

Darius, dressed in black shorts and a blue T-shirt, is standing chatting to someone near his car when I arrive outside the restaurant. His car is a gorgeous silver Audi, and the other bloke is admiring it. He acknowledges my presence, before speaking in Greek to Darius again and then heading off.

'Nice car,' I comment.

Darius thanks me and holds the passenger door open for me to step inside. A perfect gentleman.

'Top on or off?' Darius asks.

'Pardon?'

'The sunroof: open or closed.' He's grinning.

Thinking of how wild my hair would get in the wind, I opt for closed.

'Unless you want to arrive at the gardens with me looking like a crazy woman.' I point to my hair and he laughs.

'So, how are things going? You must be pleased with how well the bakery is doing,' Darius says as we drive.

'Absolutely thrilled. I couldn't have predicted how popular it would be, it's more than I could have hoped for.'

'It is just what the village needed. Everybody missed the old bakery. It seems you coming here and opening it was meant to be.'

'Do you believe in fate then?'

'Hmm. No, actually. Not really. I believe you make your own fate. When it comes to making a success in your working life, at least. I guess some things are out of our control.'

We turn away from the village onto some main roads, and just over thirty minutes later we scale a long, uphill route and arrive at the Botanical Gardens. Darius pays the entrance fee and the lady at reception hands us each a ticket and a bottle of water, along with a little map of the gardens. A pathway from the reception area leads out to the start of the walk, where I can already see huge palms in the distance, and bursts of colourful plants and foliage. Out of nowhere, a colourful bird swoops down from a tall tree.

I'm having a lovely time, strolling and chatting in such beautiful, relaxing surroundings. The gardens have plants and trees from all around the world, with little information boards beside them.

'Look at this. Gingko biloba plant.' I look at the spiky green leaves. 'It says here it's good for mental health and energy.'

There's a plant next to it, with a knobbly trunk and brown-coloured leaves, which looks unattractive but is apparently one of the most important plants in the world, its bark used in a variety of life-saving drugs.

'Almost every medicine known to mankind is derived from plants, isn't it? Painkillers, cancer treatments, even poisons used in the right amounts, and yet we continue to destroy our planet.' I sigh. 'It's crazy.'

'Now this a dangerous plant.' Darius points to a delicate-looking bush with pretty light-green leaves. 'It's a wormwood bush. But don't worry, it's only dangerous if consumed in large quantities. If administered correctly, it can be used as a stomach medicine. It is also used to make absinthe,' he says knowledgably.

'Very impressive. How come you know so much about it?' I ask.

He stands to one side and reveals the information board he has been reading, grinning to himself.

'You had me there.' I laugh.

The bush has beautiful green leaves that remind me of hands spread out.

'Looks can be so deceptive,' I remark. 'Who would think that something so attractive could be so toxic.'

'That is not just the case with plants,' Darius says as we walk on and I can't help wondering if he is referring to someone in particular.

There are so many species of plants and tall, feathery shrubs in the shadows of huge, sometimes alien-looking trees, that I feel as though I am in a distant land. An unusually marked bird, with black and white spots and red feet, walks past, with almost a Jurassic feel. I absorb the interesting facts and, passing a huge lavender bush, Darius takes some of the plant between his fingers and rubs it.

'May I?'

He moves closer, and glides his fingers over my temples, the perfume immediately hitting my nostrils.

'Good for the senses.' The feel of his hands on my skin and the intoxicating scent send me into a spin.

After walking for around an hour, we come to a green lake with peacocks strutting about. Walking on, we pass a friendly donkey in an enclosure, who approaches us, maybe hoping for some snacks, and is soon joined by a group of hopeful goats.

'Sorry, buddy, I have nothing.' I stroke the donkey's nose. In another enclosure nearby, a group of noisy chickens are clucking loudly.

We follow a wooden sign that will eventually lead us to where the restaurant is at the top of a slope. We are shown to a table on the restaurant balcony. It feels a bit like being in a tree house, giving us an all-round view of the surrounding forest. It's stunningly beautiful. A waitress hands us a menu before taking our drinks order.

'Gosh, this is so lovely. It really feels like you're getting away from everything here. Thanks for suggesting this place.'

'I'm happy you have had a nice time. I haven't been here for a while myself. Today has reminded me that I ought to spend more time with nature. I guess things have been so busy at the restaurant these summer months. Not that I am complaining!'

I notice goat curry is on the menu. I don't think I could bring myself to eat such a thing since my regular visitor appeared at the house. I have to admit it, I've become rather fond of my goat friend.

I eventually settle on a pork dish with rice and Darius orders a Cretan stew, with local sausage and vegetables. Our drinks – freshly squeezed orange juices – arrive in Kilner jars with a straw and a slice of orange at the side. As the sun warms my arms on the terrace, I feel like I could be sitting in the middle of the rainforest, especially as somewhere in the distance the sound of a squawking bird can be heard.

When the food arrives, I decide to take it as an opportunity to try out the Greek I have been practising. Then I see the look of horror on the waiter's face. Darius breaks into a smile, before conversing with the waiter in Greek.

'I take it you wanted to say the food looks appealing?' he says, barely able to contain his laughter.

'Yes, that's right,' I tell him, feeling very pleased with myself.

'Then it's a pity you told him that it looks appalling.'

'I never! Oh my goodness, I want to die of embarrassment. I must have entered the incorrect spelling into Google Translate.'

We enjoy our delicious food, the pork dish so tasty, rich with tomato and flavours of oregano and smoky peppers. The stew Darius has also looks tantalising, and I find myself looking at it jealously, wishing I had chosen the same thing.

'Are you staring at my sausage?' Darius asks.

'What? Oh, I was just having food envy,' I say, once I've stopped laughing at his remark.

'My meal is lovely, but I often think I've made the wrong choice,' I explain.

'Would you like to try some?' He lifts a small forkful of food to my mouth for me to taste.

'Mmm, it's delicious. I'll definitely order that next time I see it on a menu.' I dab my mouth with a napkin, suddenly feeling a little self-conscious.

There's a lemon cheesecake on the menu, which is my absolute favourite, so, despite feeling full, I manage a creamy, zesty slice.

The food menu states that they use the oranges and lemons grown in the gardens for the juices they make here, along with some of the herbs in the stews, which I think is wonderful.

'Did you enjoy your meal?' says the same waiter, as he clears our plates away, a smile playing around his mouth.

'Yes. And I will tell you in English, so there is no confusion. It was absolutely delicious.'

'Have you explored much of the area around the village?' Darius asks, as we enjoy our post-meal coffees.

'I've explored a few beach restaurants and been into Chania, but not many historical places. It's something I really hope to do in the future, though.'

'You know, Crete is very famous for its Nazi resistance during World War Two. There's a bunker at the top of a hill near the main street on Platanias. It's been perfectly preserved and is a small museum now. Although if you really want to look into the history, the Maritime Museum at the port of Chania is really interesting.'

I can't believe I've been here for five months and haven't been there yet, although I guess I have been busy with the house and opening up the bakery.

I settle the bill, despite his protestations. Our hands collide as we pick the tab up at the same time, and I feel another jolt of something. I wonder whether he felt it too?

'Well, that was a perfectly lovely day out, Darius, thank you,' I tell him, when we arrive back at the village, a little after three in the afternoon. 'I feel so refreshed and relaxed.'

'It was my absolute pleasure. Thank you for the lunch.'

We're standing facing each other closely for a moment, and I sense something passing between us, but then a man calls Darius's name, before crossing the street to speak to him.

'See you soon,' I tell him, before I slip away.

The sun is still warm on my skin as I walk so once I'm back home, I drag a sunbed from the storeroom and soak up the rays, its glorious warmth washing over my body. As I gather my thoughts, it occurs to me that I've been so busy this past week I haven't had time to think about Jamie. Although I do still miss him, it's mainly in the evening when I find myself alone. Right now, I think instead about the wonderful day I've just had with Darius. And wonder what his story is. He once briefly mentioned that he lived in Heraklion, but that things 'didn't work out' with someone and I wonder if he was referring to a relationship that had broken down.

In the early evening, I head to the bakery and make a load of cakes for tomorrow and, inspired by the fresh lemons and oranges at the café today, make a batch of cupcakes using lemon and orange zest. I feel fired up with enthusiasm for the future, knowing that my life is here and I want to spend every day enjoying it. I made a decision to make my life here in Crete and with every day that passes, I'm becoming more convinced it was the right thing to do.

29

I lock up and arrive home just before nine o'clock. Billy the goat is near my front door and I fish the cupcake out of my bag that I was planning on having with a hot chocolate before bed later. 'Tell me what you think. I could probably do without those calories before bedtime, anyway,' I say, as Billy stares at me blankly.

Billy gobbles it up while quickly nodding his head up and down as he eats, which makes me smile again.

'I'll take it you approve then. Goodnight,' I say, as he licks his lips before heading off into the night.

Just then, I see Eleni and Stelios getting out of their car and heading towards their house. Eleni is laughing and Stelios is walking slowly across the lawn, cursing in Greek.

'Stelios. Old man. What happened to you?' a nearby dog walker shouts across to him. He's talking in Greek, but I can just about make out his words.

Eleni replies in Greek and, upon hearing the old man's reply, she laughs loudly.

'Oh dear, are you alright?' I make my way towards them.

'I will be. I am glad my wife finds this whole business so

amusing.' He shakes his head, for once not replying with a witty riposte.

'It was just your friend.' She stifles another giggle. 'He say that you walk like you shit yourself.' She laughs once more.

'Stelios, what on earth has happened?' I ask, trying not to laugh at Eleni's infectious giggle.

'I was having a drink with Leo and playing cards. He starts reminiscing about his wrestling days. I tell him, I have some moves too. We have a little grapple, just a little fun, when suddenly I lose my balance and fall into the fire pit.'

I gasp and my hand shoots up to my mouth in shock.

'The flames had died down, of course, but it was still a little hot.'

'Oh my goodness, that must be so painful. Is there anything I can do?'

'Not unless you want to rub some ointment into his back-side. Luckily, it was not too serious. No lasting damage,' Eleni tells me, having finally stopped giggling.

Once I've stepped inside my house and closed the door, the laughter I have kept inside erupts from my body and I realise it's the first time I've belly laughed in weeks. Despite his unfortunate accident, and feeling a little sorry for him, I can't help thinking it could only happen to Stelios. I watch some television before I take myself to bed, still chuckling about poor Stelios and his burned bottom.

I wake at five o'clock the next morning, bleary eyed, to the sound of my phone ringing.

'Charlie, hi, how are you?' Milly asks.

'Just waking up, how are you? Is everything alright?' My heart is pounding in my chest wondering why my sister is ringing, thinking people only call at such early hours to deliver bad news.

'Well, no, not really. It's Jamie. I know you're not together any more but...' She pauses for a moment. 'He's had an accident.'

'An accident?' I ask as my mouth goes dry. 'What's happened?'

'It was at the garage where he's working now,' she tells me. 'He was fixing up a car when some machinery fell on top of him. The doctor's say he's critical and drifting in and out of consciousness. He's asked about you when he's been awake.'

When we finish the call, the only thing I can think about is going to see Jamie. We spent four years together, and the thought of his life hanging in the balance fills me with dread. I'd never forgive myself if something happened to him and I never got the chance to say goodbye.

Arriving at the bakery, my thoughts swirling, I tell Katerina the news.

'Oh my goodness, that is awful. What will you do?' she says, as she slides a tray of bread from the hot oven, a look of concern on her face.

'I have to go and see how he is for myself, I think, although I know it's hardly the right time to be heading back to England. Gosh, that sounds really heartless, doesn't it? What I mean is, I don't want to leave you here on your own.'

Katerina steps towards me and hugs me. 'Oh, Charlotte, you must go. You know I can manage here for a few days. I'm sure Eleni will help out too. Maybe there would not be the same selection of cakes, but people have lived without a bakery for a long time. A few more days won't make any difference,' she reassures me.

'You're right, I suppose, thanks, Kat, you're a real friend.'

Later that afternoon, I scour flights and discover that there is one from Chania Airport that leaves in two days' time and returns four days later, before the flights stop at the end of the holiday season.

I speak to Milly again and she says I can stay with her, which I'm grateful for, so I book the flights. My stomach churns when I think of Jamie lying there helpless. I just hope to God his injuries aren't life changing.

30

'I am so sorry to hear about Jamie. Please pass on our regards.'

Stelios has insisted on giving me a lift to the airport this morning so I don't need to leave my car in the car park.

'Thank you, Stelios, and for driving me here.'

We travel in relative silence and Stelios reassures me that Eleni is looking forward to working in the shop.

'She has baked some lemon cake from your recipe and some toasted almond buns, using almonds from our own tree. Eleni's almond cake is the best I have ever tasted,' he says proudly. 'I am sure your reputation will not be ruined.' He laughs loudly.

'That sounds wonderful. Thanks to both of you for your support, I really am truly grateful.'

Milly collects me from Manchester Airport and we chat as she drives me to her house to freshen up.

'Gosh, it's a terrible business, isn't it?' says Milly as we approach Chester, passing familiar landmarks on the way. 'It never crossed my mind that working with cars could be dangerous.'

It's a typical late autumn day, and we drive past trees that already have the bejewelled colours of pale yellow and orange as their leaves gently swirl to the ground. It's the first time I've been back since the move and I feel a sense of nostalgia as we drive, noting all the places I grew up with. I catch a glimpse of the city walls I used to enjoy walking along in the morning. It feels strange to think that I'm only here for a visit, yet despite the memories it evokes, I have no burning desire to return for good, so I know I have made the right decision.

An hour later, I'm being shown to a side room in the Countess of Chester Hospital, my mouth dry, wondering what I am going to find inside. I gasp when I see Jamie hooked up to an array of monitors, with machines bleeping and screens displaying numbers in red and green. Otherwise, it is silent. He looks completely unresponsive and a lonely tear rolls down my cheek.

'Oh, Jamie, what on earth has happened to you?' I weep. 'Can he hear me?' I ask the nurse who has just entered the room, as I take a seat at his bedside.

'To be honest, it's almost impossible to know. He was only conscious briefly. I believe that's when he murmured your name and asked for you.'

I take his hand in mine, but there's no response, no squeeze or indication that he can feel anything at all. Oh, Jamie. *Why couldn't we have worked things out?* I think to myself, barely able to take in what has happened to him. If he'd stayed in Greece then he'd be okay right now. But then again, he never would have stayed. He wasn't happy there; I must remember that. It was clear we wanted different things, and neither of us wanted to make a sacrifice, so perhaps our love hadn't been as strong as it appeared. For a split second, I wonder whether I have done the right thing in coming here.

I sit by Jamie, talking to him for a couple of hours. I chat about life in Greece, about small things like the difference in the weather. I tell him all about the bakery and the funny story of

Stelios falling into the fire pit. For a second, I think I see a smile play around his lips, but I'm pretty sure I am imagining things.

As I leave, the nurse tells me some more visitors will be arriving soon, including Jamie's parents. I can't imagine what they are going through right now. Although I would like to stop and say hello, I think I have maybe gone through enough emotional turmoil for one day, and suddenly feel exhausted.

That evening, Milly and I are sitting having a glass of wine. We've just said goodnight to Noah, who spent the last hour before bed making a rocket from a cardboard box and a funnel covered in foil, which was pretty impressive. Milly tells me that Noah is doing a topic about space at school, and is enjoying every minute. Milly tops up my glass and puts her arm around me again.

'God, it was awful seeing him lying there like that,' I confess, feeling drained.

'It can't have been easy for you. And poor Jamie. It's so shocking.'

'I know. I have had to try to move on these last few months, but I still care about him. I can't switch my feelings off overnight. It's all a little confusing.' I take a sip of my wine.

I tell her all about how I've met new friends, male and female, and have even been out for drinks with them.

'But mainly, it's been nice just getting to know myself again. It's so lovely waking up in the mornings, heading to the bakery, then spending my evenings exactly the way I choose to.'

'So, you never feel lonely?' she asks.

'Not any more. I think I'm alright. I have discovered that I actually like my own company, so I don't miss having a partner, if that's what you mean.'

My first love was a boy called Joe who I dated at school for three years, although it was an innocent romance by today's standards. At nineteen, I met a bloke at college and we dated for a year or two, before he broke things off. It hit me hard and I vowed to stay single forever, which lasted all of a few months. When Jamie came into my life, I thought I'd met the man I would be with forever.

'So, tell me about these men that you have been for casual drinks with,' asks Milly, her interest piqued.

I tell her about Kostas and Darius, even the morning I had fun chatting with Apollo after my kitchen ceiling caved in.

'Apollo is such good fun. I almost envy his youth – spending time at university and wondering what the future holds.'

'Would you have your time again if you could?'

'You know, I'm not sure I would. Every experience in life shapes our future, right?' I say, surprised by my own philosophical thoughts.

'So they say, although there are probably a few things I would change if I could. Anyway, it sounds like you're certainly not short on admirers, lucky you,' she says, refreshing her glass. 'It's not so easy around here, I can tell you.'

'So, you've given up on dating websites then?'

'Totally. I keep waiting for someone to walk into the library, our eyes meeting across the room as I'm stacking books of poetry on the shelves. We'll have a discussion about the great poets and he will look like someone from *Poldark*,' she says dreamily. 'I'm definitely not looking though. As I said, I'm concentrating on Noah.'

'Well, love usually finds you when you don't go looking for it. It's funny like that.'

I'm heading to bed, when a text arrives from Katerina telling me that today went well, as busy as ever, and asking how Jamie is. I tap out a reply before I settle down in Milly's spare room. Tomorrow I will head into town and visit Sue at the café before I go to the hospital again. I say a little prayer for Jamie before I settle down to sleep.

31

'Charlotte! Oh, my goodness what are you doing here?'

Sue comes from around the counter and gives me a hug.

'I came for one of your marvellous scones, of course.' I nod to the huge fluffy scones under a plastic dome. 'And a pot of English tea, too, if you wouldn't mind.' I hand her a box of baklava and she thanks me. 'Although, the real reason for my trip is to visit Jamie in hospital. Did you hear about the accident?' I ask.

'Yes, I heard about it from your sister. What an awful thing to have happened, I'm so sorry.' She gently touches my arm.

'I know, it's terrible. I went to visit him yesterday, and it was awful seeing him just lying there. But how are you? Any regrets about buying the café and giving up being a lady of leisure?'

'Not a single one. I love every minute of being here, it's given me a new lease of life. I had too many hours to fill after Colin died.'

'Well, I'm so happy things have worked out.'

The café is exactly as I remember it, although she has added a couple of prints of the river to the walls and painted the area behind the counter a pale yellow. That and one or two tweaks to the menu, but it remains pretty much the same.

'So, what's life like in Greece then?' She has joined me for a cup of tea while there's a lull in customers.

'I love it, Sue. I'm running a bakery there now. I won't lie, I was a little worried how the English cakes would go down, but they've been very well received. Apart from the Victoria sponge, interestingly, which hasn't been so popular.'

'Well, I'm glad you've settled. It's a shame things didn't work out with Jamie, but I'm glad you're happy in Greece.'

We chat for a while longer, then I finish my tea and stand to leave. 'Oh, and your scones are as fabulous as ever. I never could get mine to be as good as yours. Are you sure you don't have a secret ingredient?'

'No, just make sure you make them with love.' She smiles. 'Bye, Charlie. Thanks for the baklava. I'll try a piece after my dinner this evening. I've been craving sweet things lately, as I've given up smoking, which probably means I'll soon be fit enough to run for a bus but I'll have no teeth.'

'Bye, Sue, take care,' I say, laughing at her remark.

She waves as I set off around the corner to catch a bus to the hospital, and I start to wonder what state Jamie will be in when I arrive there today.

When I reach the ward, the nurse on duty tells me that there is another visitor sitting with Jamie, but that I am still welcome to sit with him for a while. I hesitate for a moment outside the window of the room, where the blinds are open enough for me to notice a dark-haired woman around my age sitting on a chair beside Jamie's bed. She dabs her eyes with a tissue, and I notice that she's holding his hand. I don't recognise the woman as a family member, but then I don't suppose I met *all* of Jamie's relatives, and he did once mention that some of his family were spread far and wide around the UK.

I'm considering whether I ought to go inside or not, when

the woman's eyes meet mine and she stands up. A moment later, the door opens and she stands there.

'Have you come to visit Jamie?' she asks.

'Umm, yes, but I didn't want to disturb you.'

'Not at all. Please. Are you a relative?' she asks, closing the door behind us.

'I was about to ask you the same thing funnily enough.' I laugh.

'I'm Jamie's girlfriend. My name's Natalie.'

I let the words sink in. This is Jamie's girlfriend. Suddenly I feel very silly standing here, as if I am intruding in some way. It's clear he has moved on with his life.

'I'm Charlotte,' I tell her.

'As in Charlie? His ex?'

'Yes. I heard Jamie was in a bad way, so I came over. I'll be honest, I wasn't sure if I was coming to see him for the last time. I'm sorry, maybe I should leave.'

'Don't be. I'm sure he'd appreciate you being here, but then, I'm not sure he's been aware of any of his visitors.' She sighs.

Not for the first time, I wonder whether Jamie has said my name in confusion. Perhaps he'd suffered temporary memory loss after the accident? Whatever the reason, I don't think I should be the person he wakes up to. I sit for a while talking to Natalie, who is perfectly friendly and assures me that I don't need to dash off, but I think it's for the best. As I leave, I bump into Matty, who is heading into the hospital to see his friend. He wraps me in a hug and tells me it's good to see me.

'You too. How are you?' I ask him. He looks tired.

'Worried sick. I can't stand seeing my best friend like this. We mustn't give up hope though.'

'That's the spirit. He's young and strong, I'm sure he will pull through.'

Steph has invited me around to her place tomorrow evening while Matty heads off to football. It's something Jamie would be joining him for under normal circumstances. I choke back a tear when I think of him lying there unconscious and head for the bus thinking of how your life can change in the blink of an eye.

The next evening, Steph has made us a delicious curry, which I devour in minutes. It's not something I have eaten since being in Greece.

'Gosh, thanks, Steph, I didn't think I was hungry but it is so delicious it's hard to resist,' I say, after dipping the last piece of naan bread into the creamy curry sauce.

We sip a beer each and I ask her how Matty has been since the accident.

'Awful, to be honest. He's been going to the hospital as soon as he finishes work. He felt guilty going to football training tonight, but I told him Jamie would want him to go. I think it might do him good.'

'I'm sure it will. It's just so horrible. I met his new girlfriend yesterday,' I tell Steph, who goes a little quiet.

'Matty told me he had been dating someone,' Steph says gently. 'I don't know if you'd exactly call her his girlfriend though,' she adds.

'That's how she introduced herself. Anyway, it's fine. I knew he wouldn't stay single for long. I'm glad he's moved on.'

'Are you?'

'Yes. Don't get me wrong, my feelings for Jamie haven't just disappeared instantly, but I'm getting on with my life. We made different choices and I have to respect that.'

I have a tiny slice of lemon meringue pie that Steph has bought from Waitrose, which suddenly makes me think of the lemon trees in my own garden in Greece.

'I can't wait to come over and see you again. Maybe I'll leave Matty here and we can have a girlie few days next spring,' suggests Steph.

'That sounds amazing. And I know Matty is Jamie's friend, but he is still welcome too,' I tell her. 'Although, in truth, a few days with you sounds perfect.'

I promise to call Steph in two days' time when I set off back to Crete, thankful that I have such lovely friends both here and at home.

The following day, I get news that Jamie has regained consciousness. He's still critical, but stable, and I thank God for this lifeline. I visit him as soon as I can and he groggily thanks me for coming to see him, although he seems a little surprised.

'Did you think I was going to croak?' he says, managing a smile.

'Maybe I did,' I reply honestly. 'Although it's nice to see that you're not about to.'

'I appreciate you being here. It gives me a chance to say sorry in person.'

He closes his eyes and drifts away somewhere for a second.

'You don't need to be sorry. We had four good years together but we wanted different things. I hope we can still be friends.'

Jamie reaches over and squeezes my hand.

'I'd like that, Charlie. Are you happy in Greece?' he asks sleepily.

'I am.'

'Then I'm happy too.'

'Thank you. I hope you get well soon. Bye, Jamie.'

He smiles, drifting off to sleep, as I head off.

It's my last evening with Noah and Milly tonight, and if any good has come from this, it's that I've had a chance to spend some time with my family. It's the weekend after Halloween, and there's a little event taking place near the river tonight, which I'm sure Noah will enjoy. Tomorrow I'll be heading back to my home in Greece.

'It's been lovely having you here, sis, even in the circumstances,' says Milly. She links arms with me as we walk along the river, gazing at the illuminated pumpkins adorning the decks of some of the boats. Witches and mummies pop out from behind kiosks offering sweets, much to the delight of the children who are walking with their parents. Noah has a little basket that is quickly becoming filled with sweet treats. It's chilly and I had to borrow a coat from Milly for this evening's stroll, forgetting how cold early November can be in England.

'I know. I never imagined I would be here for Halloween but seeing Noah dressed up has been a real delight. And seeing you, of course.'

There's a face painter at a stand and Noah stops and has a bat painted across his face. A stall close by is selling popcorn, toffee apples and hot drinks, so we buy hot chocolates topped with whipped cream and enjoy them seated at a bench by the river, twinkling lights shining on the water.

As we stroll, ghosts, zombies and witches continue to walk by, entertaining the children.

Later, back at home, we play bobbing for apples with Noah and his little friend from next door, which they find highly amusing, giggling as they come up for air.

'I remember you trying to drown me when we played that as a kid,' I tell Milly, which she hotly denies.

'Never! I would just give you a gentle push as you'd never put your face fully in the water.'

'If you say so.'

We head to bed, and I find myself lying awake for a while thinking about Jamie. I'm glad I came to see him: I'm relieved that it would appear he will make a full recovery, but also that I feel I've laid a ghost to rest. I'd been wondering lately if he had any regrets about coming back to Chester, but it seems that isn't the case and I feel good about that. In fact, seeing him with someone else didn't make me feel jealous, reinforcing the fact that I made the right decision about my future. We are both getting on with our new lives, and I actually feel quite satisfied knowing that.

32

It's a warm evening when I disembark and head towards the taxi rank at Chania Airport, feeling good to be home.

I call Katerina. She's at the village bar, so I head over there for a drink.

'Charlotte. Good to see you. How was England?'

'Nippy. I had to borrow a coat from my sister.'

She gives a little shiver at the thought.

She's with her mum and aunt, having a drink for her aunt's birthday. She gestures for me to sit, orders us some more wine, and then proceeds to tell me all about the wonderful meal they've just enjoyed at The Fig Tree.

'And soon it's time for my bed.' She glances at her watch; it's almost ten o'clock.

'Mine too.' I stifle a yawn as I take the last sip of my rather nice glass of Merlot.

'How's it been then? I'm afraid it's a little late for me to have any cakes ready for tomorrow, so I'm hoping your bread is still selling like hot cakes. If you know what I mean.'

She laughs. 'Don't worry, I knew that. Eleni and I have

made baklava, scones and walnut cake. Oh and a coconut and almond bun. I found the recipe online and tried it out yesterday on my mother. She declared it a success, and she is a harsh critic.'

'Thank you, Katerina. I don't know what I would do without you.'

'So how is Jamie?' she asks as we walk out of the door together.

I fill her in with the story, telling her that he seems to have a new girlfriend.

'I'm relieved that he is going to be alright, and we left it saying we should still be friends, although I don't know what that means exactly. It's not as if we've been in touch since we split, so I'd say that's the end of that chapter in my life.'

Saying it out loud, I feel a weight has been lifted from my shoulders. I have fully immersed myself into my new life in Crete, and just as I told Milly, I am happily rediscovering myself again. Being in a relationship would only complicate things right now.

'Morning, Stelios. You're walking a little easier now,' I say with a laugh. 'How are things?'

My neighbour has called into the bakery the next morning for bread, looking a little sprightlier.

'Better,' he says. 'Lots of cold baths and a swimming ring to sit on.' He chuckles, obviously managing to see the funny side of things now. 'How is everything with you?'

'Good, thanks, Stelios.'

'And Jamie? I hope everything went okay?'

'It did thank you. I think he's going to be alright. I gave him your best wishes and he returned them.'

'You know, I am still sorry for the way things turned out. He was a good man, but I am sure you will have plenty of admirers in the village. In fact, I know it.'

'What do you mean? You're telling me I have a secret admirer?'

'Nothing. Maybe I say too much already.' He laughs.

Stelios takes two of the coconut and almond slices baked by Katerina. These seem to be a big hit, so will definitely stay on the menu.

'I may ask you to bake some of these for a party,' he says. 'And, of course, your lemon cake, and the walnut cake, in fact maybe everything you sell, it's all so delicious.'

'Ooh, a party. What's the occasion?' I ask, intrigued.

'Eleni's sixtieth birthday is coming up. But shush.' He puts a finger to his lips.

'A surprise party! How exciting.'

'I hope I am doing the right thing.' For a moment he looks a little uncertain. 'She did tell me that she didn't want a fuss. I worry she may kill me. I am trying to make things up to her, as she did not seem as happy with the wooden carving of her as I hoped she would be.'

'I'm sure she will love a party. Women often say they don't want a fuss, when in fact they mean the exact opposite.'

'Why not just say what you really want?' says Stelios, scratching his head.

'Oh, I don't know, something about men and women being from different planets, I guess.'

Stelios looks even more puzzled, which makes me laugh.

'Don't worry, Stelios, I'm sure she will appreciate the gesture and the trouble you have gone to. I guess it's just that most women don't like to broadcast their age, that's all.'

'We all get older, but to me she still looks beautiful. You should be proud of your age. Would rather someone think I look good for my age than whispering behind my back that I must have had a very hard life.' He laughs loudly.

'Okay, well, give me some numbers for the party as soon as possible. I'm sure Eleni will have a great time.'

'Thank you. It goes without saying you are invited. Our guest of honour, in fact.'

That afternoon, Katerina and I have arranged a shopping trip to Chania as I think I would like to treat myself to a couple of new dresses, which seems fitting now that a party is on the horizon. After a quick shower, I collect her and we head off from the village.

'I think I may need a double espresso before I start shopping,' I tell her, stifling a yawn.

'Early mornings taking their toll, are they?' Katerina laughs.

'I think they are. I really should try and have a siesta in the afternoon.'

'If you have an early start, you must have an afternoon nap,' she advises. 'Although I admit it is easier in the height of summer when the heat saps your energy.'

Katerina looks pretty today in a floaty blue skirt, white T-shirt, and a black linen blazer thrown over the top. She eyes my sleeveless pink cotton dress, saying she thinks it is a little cool this afternoon.

'It's still warm to me. Maybe I haven't quite acclimatised!'

It's early November and I'm surprised at just how good the weather is, the sun still pleasantly warm with bright blue skies. Although I enjoyed my time back in Chester, it reminded me of just how cold and dark it gets and I could barely wait to return to the sunshine here.

We find a car park and head to a café overlooking the water, giving us a view of the lighthouse. We each order coffees, an Americano for me and a cappuccino for Katerina.

'Just to give me a boost for shopping. We'll find somewhere nice for lunch later.'

'So, tell me, has there been any progress with Ralf whilst I've been away?' I ask, as I sip the strong Americano.

'If you mean has he asked me out, then no. Not even close. He came into the bakery every day for bread, but that was it. I'm not even sure that he likes me any more.' She sighs.

'Oh, I can assure you he does. I was there when he and Apollo were at the bar saying how attractive you were.'

'But he hasn't done anything about it. Maybe he has found a girlfriend since he said that.' She tosses her hair over her shoulder, making me think that Ralf would be mad if that were the case.

I never realised Ralf was quite so shy around women and wonder whether a little matchmaking may be on the cards.

Strolling through the cobbled streets of the port, we pass clothes shops, many with red posters in the windows announcing their sales. The sun appears to be getting stronger as the day progresses and Katerina removes her blazer, folding it over her arm as we stroll in the sun. There are quite a number of people out today enjoying the sunshine, taking advantage of the summer sales and stopping for ice creams at stalls that sell a variety of flavours. We stop and try on discounted sun hats and sunglasses, and I treat myself to one of each before noticing a stall outside a shop displaying my one weakness: leather bags in an assortment of colours.

'Do I really need another bag?' I say as I run my hands over a soft, tan-coloured leather handbag.

'Who said anything about need? If you like it, buy it,' Katerina says encouragingly, and before I know it, I have headed inside to pay. There's an array of soft leather purses displayed on a shelf inside as well, and I select a green one along with the bag.

'You're a bad influence,' I say when I come out of the shop.

Passing a bookshop, I spot a couple of books in English that I'd been meaning to read, so stock up on three novels to cuddle up with when the winter evenings draw in. I've always loved reading.

An hour later, I've purchased a cut-price, floaty knee-length dress in shades of turquoise and teal and Katerina has bought herself some silver earrings, a floaty white top and a new pair of jeans.

'Are you ready for something to eat now? I'm famished,' Katerina says.

'Lead the way,' I reply, so Katerina takes us down a maze of alleys, until we are finally seated outside a restaurant with thick white walls and a side sea view of the port.

'I always come here when I'm in Chania. The food is simply wonderful,' Katerina tells me, just as a waitress appears, brandishing a menu before taking our drinks order. We dine on a delicious lamb casserole, rich with the favours of rosemary and tomato, and dotted with soft, salty olives. It's served with soft pitta bread. Afterwards, we manage a small portion of warm filo pastry apple pie with a dollop of vanilla ice cream.

'Well, that was delicious. You were right to recommend this restaurant. I'm amazed I haven't gone up a dress size since living here.'

'Yes, but it is healthy food. Crete is an organic island, most of the food is farmed or grown here.'

There is evidence of that everywhere: the fishermen bringing in their haul at the quayside, the sheep farms and abundance of fruit trees covering the landscape that grow olives, figs and lemons. Not to mention grapes and almonds.

It's almost seven o'clock when we arrive back at the village, the sun already setting as a slight coolness descends on the air. I take my cardigan from the back seat of the car and wrap it around me. I'm about to head inside when I hear someone call my name.

I turn around to find Apollo, walking through the garden gate.

'Apollo, hi. I didn't realise you were still in town. I thought you would have gone back to university by now,' I say, surprised to see him here.

He stands with his hands in his pockets and shrugs.

'Actually, do you have any free time? I would like to take you for a drink and ask your advice, if you don't mind too much.'

I'm pretty exhausted and I have a little baking to do, but I can see he is in need of a listening ear.

'Sure, just let me get my shopping inside,' I say, lifting my bags.

Ten minutes later, we're sitting at the local bar sipping beers.

'So, what's on your mind then?' I ask. Apollo has the look of someone wrestling with his emotions.

'University has been in my thoughts a lot this past week. I think I have some decisions to make.' He drinks his beer.

'What kind of decisions?'

He is quiet for a minute before he speaks.

'I'm not sure I want to continue at university,' he reveals. 'But I don't have the nerve to tell my father.'

'Aren't you enjoying university life?' I ask, a little surprised.

'University life, yes. I have made some good friends, and even had one or two girlfriends, but I do not want to be a doctor any more.'

'Do you think you would be suited to something else?'

'I would like to be an artist, but I know my father would never accept that. Funny really, as I get my talent from him. He is very creative, especially with wood carving.'

I think back to the day Steph and I saw the sculpture he was working on in his shed and Eleni's reaction to it.

'Surely he would understand, if you tell him where your heart really is?' I reason.

'No. It was always his dream to become a doctor, but he never had the opportunity as a young man. He has helped me so much to have this chance. I was a natural at sciences at school, which he saw as a sign. He is so proud. He tells everyone in the village that I am going to be a doctor. I feel like I cannot let him down.' He swirls his beer around and sighs.

'Your father won't be the first parent to try and live their dreams through their child, but the reality is, it's your life. I'm pretty sure he won't disown you for doing what you truly want.'

'I wish that were true.'

'Maybe it is. You'll never know until you speak to him. You might even be overthinking things. I'm sure your parents would be sadder at the thought of you being unhappy.'

'I suppose that's true. I've been putting off talking to him.'

'You should speak to your parents as soon as possible. Especially if you are thinking of doing something completely different.'

'I know. You are right, of course. It is my life and I should be doing what makes me happy. I feel better just talking about it. Thank you, Charlotte.'

He heads to the bar, before returning with two glasses of red wine.

'Let's drink to change, and being happy.' We clink our glasses together.

'Well, my life has certainly changed these past few months, so I'll definitely drink to that.'

As we sip our wine, a smile spreads across Apollo's face.

'I'm glad you came to live here in the village,' he says sincerely.

'Me too,' I reply, thinking I have found another genuine friend. 'Me too.'

Walking home just after ten, pleasantly relaxed after a few glasses of wine, and laughing loudly at something Apollo has just said, I notice Darius stacking chairs outside his restaurant, preparing to close up for the evening. I'm certain he sees me too, so I raise my hand and wave, but he carries on with the chairs before heading inside the restaurant, and switching off the lights.

33

The next morning I'm at the bakery just after six, putting some raspberry buns and chocolate brownies into the oven, along with some walnut cake. Katerina's baklava is popular, and she's been adding pistachios, cranberries and figs, which have gone down a storm.

'I think I had better make some more of those buns today,' she says, taking some baguettes from the oven.

I'd suggested Katerina make some cheesy crusty rolls, a big hit in the café in Chester, which have proved popular here too.

We're grabbing a quick coffee later, once the breadbaskets are filled and trays of cakes placed under the glass, when I tell Katerina about Darius.

'I'm pretty sure he saw me, we made eye contact, yet he went inside and closed the door.'

'You can't be sure he noticed you as it would have been dark by then. Why would he ignore you?' she asks, sipping her coffee.

'I'm not sure. I've been wondering if I've done something to offend him. Oh, I don't know, maybe he was just tired.' I shrug and decide to forget all about it.

It's another busy morning; the cheese rolls are selling out so fast Katerina thinks she will have to make even more tomorrow. Just before three, we close up as usual, with just a couple of loaves and two chocolate brownies left in stock.

'I think I'll take one of these for later,' I say, popping a brownie into a bag. 'You take the other.'

Instead of heading home, I feel like some fresh air and find myself walking towards the beach, determined to make the most of the sunny days here in Crete.

The waves are crashing gently against the rocks today, and I head down to the far end of the beach where the boat trips leave. A small group of holidaymakers are stepping aboard a blue and white glass-bottomed boat called the *Princess* and, on impulse, I decide to purchase a ticket and join them. Taking a seat on the boat, I can feel the wind blowing through my hair and I inhale the fresh, salty sea air, lifting my face to the sun as it beats down. A passenger has just pointed to a shoal of silvery fish below the glass floor of the boat, when suddenly a large squid swims amongst them and people snap away with their cameras in delight.

An hour later, returning to the bay, I feel completely refreshed, and wonder why I haven't taken a boat trip since I've been here. I resolve to do more next summer, maybe heading out to other parts of the island.

Walking through the village later, I bump into Ralf as he steps out of his car, returning from his job in Chania. He looks smart in a light grey suit.

'Ralf! Hi, how are things?'

'Hi, Charlotte. Good, thanks, although I feel a little sick.'

'Are you ill?' I ask, puzzled, thinking he looks like a picture of health.

'No, it is my nerves. I have made up my mind I will ask Katerina out.'

'Do you have her number?'

'No. I know where she lives, though. But maybe I will wait until tomorrow morning. I can see her at the bakery before I head to work,' he decides. 'Do you think she will say yes?' he asks nervously.

'Let's just say I don't think you have anything to worry about. Just ask her,' I reassure him.

Ralf leaves looking happy, and I wonder whether I ought to give Katerina a heads up. I decide against it. It's more romantic if these things happen naturally.

I spot Stelios walking with Apollo along the village, heading towards the local bar, and I wonder whether Apollo is going to talk of his wish to change courses at university. I do hope things go well for him. I'm living proof that we should all do what makes us happy in life – our life is precious. Our life is our own.

On my way home a text arrives from Steph telling me Jamie is making good progress and the doctors are hopeful he will make a full recovery. I wish him nothing but the best. I've accepted my new life here now, and as I open the gate to my pretty house and garden, something tells me I'm going to be okay.

I spot Darius the following morning, out walking alone as I head to the bakery for a morning's work.

'*Kalimera*, Darius, you are up and about early,' I remark, as it's only just after six.

'*Kalimera*. Yes, I had a restless sleep last night.'

'Is everything okay?'

'I think so. Just something I have to make a decision about.'

Maybe that explains why he was lost in his own thoughts last night.

We fall into step as we walk and he tells me he has discovered he has an inheritance: an aunt has left a large restaurant in the port of Chania to him and Kostas. In her will, she states she would love the restaurant to continue in the hands of Darius, although if Kostas wants to sell, she will understand.

'It leaves me with a dilemma. The restaurant is the most beautiful place, in a prime location overlooking the lighthouse. My aunt never had any children of her own, so Kostas and I are her next of kin,' he explains.

'It would be quite a change from the village,' I say, suddenly realising how strange it would feel not to speak to Darius most days. 'Although I must admit, I would miss seeing you around.' To my surprise, the thoughts that were in my head have come out of my mouth.

'Would you really?' He turns to face me, a serious look on his face.

'Of course I would. I enjoy our chats.'

'I thought that maybe I was just one of many men you speak to,' he muses.

'I beg your pardon?' I say, shocked by his remark.

'Sorry, I do not mean to offend, it's just, it's not as if you don't have other men here to keep you company, is it?'

'What are you getting at?' I ask, aghast.

'Well, I have seen you in bars with my brother and young Apollo.' He seems to emphasise the word young. 'So I thought that maybe I was no one special, as you are not short of admirers in the village.'

'Admirers? Hardly! They're just friends,' I tell him, wondering why I am even explaining myself.

'I am sorry.' He lifts his hands. 'I think what I said may have come out wrong. I did not mean to upset you.'

'Well, you did.' So he thinks he is one of *many* men I speak to? 'I got to know your brother through his work on the annexe, which you are well aware of. Apollo is the son of my neighbour. They are nothing more than friends.' I feel stung by his remark. Does he perceive me as some kind of floozy, accepting drinks from all the available men in the village? Suddenly I can feel tears threatening.

'I think I should be going now.'

'Charlotte, please, I apologise.'

I can hear his words, but I am striding on towards the shop, leaving him standing there in the middle of the street, his hands laced behind his head.

34

Katerina and I arrive at the shop at the same time, and I fumble for my key to open the door.

'Good morning. Are you alright?' asks Katerina as we enter the shop.

'Yes, fine.' I plaster a smile on my face. 'Just a little rushed this morning, that's all.'

We have a lot of work to do, so I decide to keep Darius's comments to myself. For now, at least.

Halfway through the morning service, Stelios arrives brandishing a list.

'For the party, in four weeks' time. Forty people, if that is okay? Seven thirty at the bar.'

I chat with him about food, and he asks me to arrange a selection of my cakes, as well as sandwiches, breads and dips.

'If our buffet is a success at the party, maybe events are something we could get into,' says Katerina as she serves an elderly woman dressed in black. 'My friend Selina runs a small café in the next village, but business is a little slow at the moment. She has been thinking about doing some outside catering.'

'Well, that's definitely something to think about. And having an extra pair of hands would be good.' I vow to give the idea some thought.

The day passes quickly and soon enough we are locking up. I think about my meeting with Darius this morning and wonder if I overreacted. But then, why would he comment on the company I have kept with other men? Surely, he has no right to make a comment like that? As I walk, I find myself thinking about the day we spent at the Botanical Gardens once more and how relaxed and happy we both felt. If I close my eyes, I can still recall the moment our fingers touched when we reached for the bill. It stirred something inside of me, which, of course, I chose to ignore.

I feel the need to continue walking on out of the village, and fifteen minutes later, I find myself on the main street of Platanias. The road is fairly busy with some out-of-season tourists browsing the shops and sitting outside cafés, soaking up the sunshine before they head home.

Halfway up the road, I glance upwards as a sign shows directions to the World War Two bunker up above the high street. I purchase a bottle of water from a nearby kiosk, and decide to take a hike up the steep road to have a little look. Darius flits into my mind once more, as I recall him telling me it was worth a visit. The Greek resistance in Crete is well documented as being one of the bravest confrontations against Hitler's Nazi regime; the Cretans fought fiercely to keep their independence.

I can feel the pull on the back of my calves as I ascend the hill, and soon enough the tiny museum looms into view. Once inside, I realise it's little more than a tiny shelter. I'm amazed to discover that the museum has underground tunnels that were, unbelievably, dug out from the rare soft rock by a handful of men in just six months.

It pulls at my emotions to read the information boards that

reveal the shelter was constructed by Cretan troops on Platanias Hill. It was used as a bunker and had a lookout turret that gave views of Chania Bay to spot invading armies, as well as underground booths and tunnels where the locals could hide. The bunker housed ammunition during World War Two, and has been preserved as a museum, displaying photographs, guns and soldiers' outfits. There's a sombre yet peaceful feel about the small place, and although I find it compelling, it's a relief when I emerge outside once more, breathing in the fresh air.

'The building of the shelter is related to an interesting local story,' says an Englishman wearing a linen shirt, casual trousers and a camera around his neck, as we both stand viewing a battle tank.

I realise he is speaking to me and turn to face him. 'Really?'

'Yes, during the battle of Crete a wounded German pilot died here in Platanias, despite the locals nursing him.'

'Looking after the enemy. Human nature at its kindest,' I say.

'Indeed. Anyway, they buried him in a secret grave near the church, as they feared Nazi reprisals and the slaughter of innocent people,' he tells me knowledgably.

'So, what happened?' I ask, now captivated by the tale.

'Would you believe, just a few days later, the exact spot was chosen by a German officer to begin excavations to build the shelter.'

'Oh no. How strange. The exact spot?'

'Yes, very strange. Anyway, a church commissioner persuaded the officer to move the building work further along, thus concealing the soldier's grave. Luckily the officer agreed.'

'Wow. That must have been a tense time.' I listen with interest.

'Most certainly. Moving the building work and keeping it a secret will have saved the village from certain massacre.' He snaps away with his camera at the battle tank in front of us.

I thank the tourist, before making my way down the hill back to the high street, absorbing the information from the visitor, who clearly has a love of the local history.

I stop at a café down in Platanias before I head back to the village, all the while pondering how different the place must have looked during the war years. Darius was right when he said the hut was worth a visit. I've been here for months now and it's the first time I've really delved into the history of the area and now resolve to do some more.

35

Arriving at work the next morning, I find Ralf pacing up and down outside the shop, chewing his nails.

'Ralf, hi! How long have you been here?'

'Only a few minutes. I know the shop is not open yet, but I wanted to speak with Katerina before she is busy with customers.'

'No problem.' I fumble with my keys and let him in. A shocked-looking Katerina is just taking some bread rolls from the oven, so I discreetly head into the back of the kitchen to give them some privacy.

Five minutes later, I hear the door of the shop close, and Katerina gives out a little squeal.

'Someone's happy,' I comment.

'I'm going out on a date with Ralf, but I guess you already know that.' She can't stop smiling as she places a tray of bread rolls in the oven.

'What? Me? Of course I didn't. Well, I knew he might ask you out.' I tell her all about our conversation yesterday.

'You should have told me he was going to call in, then I

might not have had flour in my hair and jam on my apron,' she says, pointing to herself.

'He still asked you out, didn't he?'

'Yes! He did!' she says excitedly. 'I can hardly wait for tonight. We're going to watch an action film in Chania then have some dinner.'

Katerina spends the rest of the morning beaming and when one elderly customer asks her if she is in love she blushes like a teenager.

'Why on earth would you think that?' she asks the old gentleman after she has handed him his change.

'Because you have given me more money than I gave you for the bread.' He smiles as he hands back a ten-euro note to a shocked Katerina who apologises and thanks him for his honesty.

'And also, I can see the twinkle in your eyes.' He turns to his wife. 'My love had that look in her eyes fifty years ago when I first asked her out.'

The old lady nudges him gently and they both laugh as they leave the shop, obviously still in love after all these years. I find myself wondering if living in a place like this makes marriages last longer. Surrounded by a supportive community, and desiring little more than family and friendship. Not that they don't have fun, of course, there's plenty of parties and get-togethers, but there doesn't seem to be a desire to chase so many material possessions. Or maybe that's just with the older generation, as many younger people leave the village in search of something more. I suddenly think of Apollo and wonder whether he has spoken to his parents about his dilemma with university. If he has, then Stelios hasn't mentioned anything, which is unlike him.

Later that day, I call Milly, feeling the need to talk to her.

'Charlie, hi. Give me two minutes. I'm just giving Noah something to eat, he always comes home from school ravenous.'

'Gosh, I'd forgotten about the time difference, call me back when you've eaten.'

I busy myself tidying around and thinking about what I might have for my own dinner later, when, soon enough, Milly returns my call.

'So, how are things going?' she asks.

'All good. Stelios has asked me to do the catering for a party next month. It's Eleni's sixtieth birthday.' I tell her all about Stelios trying to keep it a secret.

'Ooh that sounds like fun, wish I was there.'

'I'm sure you'd be more than welcome if you were.'

'Nice idea, but I don't have any holiday time left. Besides, the flights will be easing off then, won't they? Never mind. So, tell me, how are all those single guys in the village?' she asks.

I find myself telling Milly all about Darius and his recent comments to gauge her reaction.

'I was absolutely fuming. I mean, where does he think he gets off, telling me who I should and shouldn't see?'

'Have you thought that he might be jealous?' she suggests.

'It did occur to me... But then, that's hardly an attractive quality in a man, is it?'

'Maybe not when you're in a relationship, no, but perhaps he's just worried you might be snapped up by someone else. Gosh. How would it make you feel if he was interested in you?' she asks.

'Confused. I know I need to move on with my life but, well, I'm scared of jumping into a new relationship, I suppose. Besides, I have enough on my plate with the shop.'

'But you are attracted to him?'

'I suppose I am. And perhaps it was a little display of jealousy on his part... I don't know.'

'You are allowed a little fun, you know. All work and no play isn't good for anyone.'

'I know. But even if I did like him, he's considering a move to Chania.'

I tell her all about the restaurant left to him by his aunt.

'It's a half hour drive away,' she says with a laugh.

'I know. Anyway, that's enough about me, how's your love life going?'

'Well, I wouldn't have said anything just yet but since you've asked,' she says enthusiastically. 'I've been out on a couple of dates with someone! I was going to give you a ring at the weekend and fill you in. I was kind of avoiding men altogether, but then fate stepped in.'

'Oh my goodness, Milly, that's great, tell me everything!'

Milly recounts a day when she was restocking the library shelves and a man with dark curly hair, dressed smartly in a grey woollen coat, spotted her placing a Walt Whitman book of poetry onto a shelf.

'His eyes widened when he saw the book. He said Walt Whitman was his favourite poet,' she chatters excitely. 'I told him he was mine too. My shift was almost over, so we grabbed a coffee nearby and discussed the merits of *Leaves of Grass*.'

'*Leaves of Grass*?'

'A collection of Whitman's most celebrated works.'

'Sorry, I'm such a philistine when it comes to poetry, or any of the classics really.' My reading choices have always alternated between romcoms and edge-of-your-seat crime thrillers. 'And, oh my gosh! I can hardly believe you met a man in the library, exactly the way you wanted to.' I can't help laughing thinking about this.

'Anyway,' she carries on, 'his name is Simon. He's divorced with a son the same age as Noah who he sees regularly. We took them both to the zoo last weekend, and they got on like a house on fire. He has such a lovely way with children. It's early days, but I have a really good feeling about this.'

'How long has he been divorced?' I can't help asking.

'Just over a year, having been separated for two years previously. His son was very young at the time, but his wife cheated on him with a colleague, who she's now living with. He's very much over it all now, so don't worry about me being a rebound romance.'

'In that case, I'm thrilled for you, I really am. He sounds like a lovely man.'

'Thanks, sis.'

We wrap up the call, with Milly telling me to keep her posted on any progress with Darius. As I'm hanging up, Leo waves to me through the window, signalling that he's about to leave. He's spent the morning once again raking the leaves into piles and disposing of them. The garden is looking neat and tidy, although the colourful blooms in the pots are beginning to wither slightly as the cooler weather approaches.

'Would you like me to empty and cover the pool next week?' asks Leo, as he sets his gardening tools into the shed. 'The weather is cooling now, and I've had to fish a few leaves out of the water today.'

I think about the last time I took a dip in the pool, over a week ago now.

'Yes, I think so, Leo, that would be great. Although the weather is still warm to me, I'm probably not going to be swimming any day soon.'

I'm still wearing a short-sleeved summer dress and take in Leo's appearance of denim shirt, trousers, and grey hair tucked into a cap. The days for swimming may be few and few far between in the coming months, and I always have the beach a short walk away. Maybe I'll become one of those people who swim in the sea on Christmas Day, or even go wild swimming in lakes. Living here, I'm beginning to believe that anything is possible.

36

The next morning, I'm heading to the local supermarket when I hear someone calling my name. I turn around to see Darius jogging up the road towards me.

'I don't feel like talking right now,' I tell him, walking on.

'Well, that's good, because you only have to listen. Please, I want to apologise.' He falls in step beside me as we walk. 'I realise you can see who you want; it is none of my business. Maybe I felt... well, perhaps I was a little jealous,' he confesses.

'I don't know what you meant by seeing someone else. I've only just split with Jamie. I was happy to be making new friends in the village, nothing more.'

'I know. I was just surprised by how I felt when I saw you with another man. Maybe I mistakenly thought you and I had a connection.'

He moves closer and despite myself, I feel my heart rate quicken. It brings to mind the day at the Botanical Gardens where the touch of his hand sent a shiver through my body.

'But,' he continues, 'I realise it was selfish of me to think that way. I know you have only recently separated from Jamie. It's just that I enjoyed spending time with you and I longed to be with you more, but I was busy with the restaurant.'

Not too busy to be going off somewhere with the waitress, I think to myself.

We stand awkwardly for a moment, my brain trying to process what Darius has just revealed, when the unmistakeable tones of Stelios ring through the air.

'Darius! Just the man. Saturday the twenty-fifth at the village bar, a party for Eleni. You are most welcome.'

He's wearing a loud yellow T-shirt, a pair of joggers and trainers on his feet.

'Thank you, Stelios. Do you want me to do anything?' he offers.

'Well, our friend here has the food under control but maybe you could make your delicious chicken casserole, the best in the village! And please send me the bill.'

'It would be my pleasure. A gift from me.'

'Right, I must be going, I am trying for ten-thousand steps along the beach today. Eleni tells me I am getting a little fat.' He roars with laughter and pats his stomach before he heads off.

'I must be going too. I'll see you later,' I say.

'Will I really see you later?' Darius places his hand gently on my arm as his gaze meets mine. His touch gives me a warm, fuzzy feeling. 'Maybe after work, I could take you out to dinner to apologise for how rude I was. I know a place near the beach that is still open,' he says hopefully.

'That might be nice,' I find myself agreeing and he tells me he will collect me at seven.

I walk away, my thoughts swirling. There is no doubt Darius's presence evokes something in me that I have previously pushed away as I thought it too soon after my break-up. But now that he's considering moving away from the village it's hardly the time to pursue a new relationship. And it wasn't part of my plan to date again; I intended to focus on the bakery and make a success of the shop. But still, something about his presence stirs a strong feeling in me.

Back at the bakery, it's a busy morning. Katerina's cheesy rolls are still going down a storm, as are the chocolate brownies. During a quiet spell, I nip to the shop next door for some bottled water, as Stelios walks past, red-faced and clutching his own water bottle.

'Did you make the ten-thousand steps then?' I ask.

'Almost. I am not fit. Eleni is right, I must lose some weight.'

He sits on the stone wall surrounding the olive tree and breathes deeply.

'Well, don't overdo it. Build your fitness up slowly,' I advise.

I'm about to leave, when Stelios tells me all about Apollo and his desire to study art.

'And what do you think about that?' I ask, taking a seat beside him on the wall.

'To tell you the truth, I was disappointed. But there is no denying my son's talent. He has been working on a portrait of his mother that is simply wonderful.' He takes a glug of his water. 'But he has such a good brain too.' He taps his head.

'Then he is lucky to have the choice of what he wants to do. But I believe that if you do something you truly love, your life will be more fulfilled. Don't they say that if you choose a job you love, you will never have to work a day in your life?'

Stelios nods slowly. 'I suppose it is true. I worked hard when I was young as a train driver. I travelled all across Greece. It was a good job that paid well, but I wanted to be a sculptor. My father, though, he thought it was not a real job. I should encourage Apollo to follow his dreams. Thank you, Charlotte.'

Walking back into the shop, I can't help wondering how many life decisions we make to seek our parents' approval, or because they are the sensible choice, rather than pursuing the thing our heart desires.

Inside, Katerina is standing behind the counter with a dreamy look on her face.

'Ralf has just texted me. He wants to take me out again for an early dinner,' she moons.

Their first date in Chania had gone well, despite an unexpected, and rather graphic, sex scene in the film they were watching. It had mortified Ralf and embarrassed Katerina, so they'd made an early exit to a bar for a cocktail.

'That sounds lovely. And as tomorrow is Sunday, do you fancy a coffee and a walk somewhere? With all the customers, we never have a chance to talk properly in here. I can tell you more about the date!'

I don't tell her that I have a date too, because, well, I'm not sure that it even is one. Maybe it's simply Darius wanting to apologise to me. Whatever it is, I find myself thinking about what to wear for the rest of the day.

I settle on a V-neck midi dress in shades of mustard and teal that emphasises my small waist and shapely figure. I let my blonde curly hair loose and I'm just applying some lip gloss when I hear a message ping through on my phone. It's from Jamie.

Thanks for coming to see me at the hospital. It meant a lot to me. I think about you a lot. Jamie. X

I pour myself a glass of wine, and sit in the kitchen pondering a reply. These past two months, I have done all I can to push thoughts of Jamie from my mind, and now he's telling me that he thinks about me. What is he trying to say? I glance at a photo of us that remains on the lounge wall, laughing on the beach in Chania, and a flood of memories come rushing back. The fun times we had with Matty and Steph, both here and at home, are pushed to the forefront of my mind. It suddenly doesn't feel right that the photo is still displayed on the wall, so I remove it and place it in a cupboard, not quite ready to consign it to the dustbin.

Eventually, I text back asking him how he is feeling, and he tells me he is almost completely better and returning to work soon. I tell him I'm happy for him. His last text simply reads *Can I call you?*

I glance at my watch. It's a little before seven. Darius will be collecting me any minute now. I tell him I'm just on my way out and he replies with a heart and arranges to call me tomorrow evening instead.

I spritz myself with some perfume, feeling completely dazed and confused. Is he having regrets about moving back to England? And what about his girlfriend? Or maybe she was someone when he was just on the rebound, who knows. I've thrown myself so much into my work in an effort to get over my heartbreak, and I thought I had succeeded. I've even allowed myself to have a flicker of attraction to someone else. But what if Jamie and I are really meant to be together? Now that he's recovered, does he think he might have made a huge mistake in returning to England? How would I feel if he did? I wish he'd never texted me and I'm lost in my confused thoughts, when I hear a knock on the front door.

Darius is standing before me, looking handsome in a shirt with a very similar colour scheme to my dress, and we both burst out laughing.

'I think I had better go home and change my shirt,' he says, before presenting me with the beautiful bunch of flowers he is holding.

'Oh, Darius, thanks, they're gorgeous.'

I place the flowers into a vase and we head to his restaurant. Darius slips inside to change, but not before a waiter spots us and grins at the sight of us dressed in the same colours.

'Better?' He appears in a crisp white shirt that complements his black jeans. Taking in his appearance, I realise he really is the most good-looking man and I feel another jolt of attraction for him as we head off.

'Are you alright?' he asks as we walk, probably noting I am a little quiet.

'What? Yes, I'm fine. Just a little tired,' I say, plastering a smile on my face and deciding not to mention Jamie, as I don't want to ruin our evening. Besides, first I need to hear what Jamie has to say for himself when he calls tomorrow.

We take a side road towards the beach as dusk falls and lights come on everywhere. Heading towards the beach, I can hear the crashing of the waves, a sound that soothes me, no matter what time of day.

The bar has lights strung along the front, and coloured tables and chairs on a wooden deck that leads to an indoor space. It's the only remaining beach bar not closed up for the season, open for locals at the weekends.

'This is beautiful.'

'I think so too,' says Darius as he pulls a seat out for me to sit down. There are various plants dotted about in metal pots painted in a Moroccan design, and stripy rugs are thrown on the floor, along with huge squashy sofas and low tables. There's a buzz about the place that I hadn't expected.

'The locals congregate here at the weekend,' Darius continues. 'The owner, Maria, is determined to keep the restaurant open for as long as possible,' he tells me, just as a smiling middle-aged woman with dark, grey-streaked hair and smiling brown eyes appears.

'*Kalispera*,' she says handing us a menu.

'*Kalispera*. I didn't realise you were still open,' I tell her, glancing around at the busy restaurant.

'Yes.' She laughs. 'I am not good at resting in the winter. I think maybe I do not like my own company. And it is possible to sit outside still. Although one year in December, a freak wave almost drowned the diners who wanted to sit outside and watch the moonlight.'

'I bet that wasn't the romantic date they imagined then,' I say, as Darius orders a bottle of wine, and she walks away smiling.

'What do you fancy then?' I bury my head in the menu.

'Are you talking about the menu?' Darius has that playful look on his face again, as he looks me in the eye.

'Do you know, you are a terrible flirt,' I tell him, closing the menu, having decided on lamb *kleftiko*.

'Me?' Darius has a look of mock shock on his face 'I wouldn't say I was a flirt, but maybe you bring that out in me.'

A waiter returns with a bottle of red wine and Darius pours us each a glass.

'So, tell me a little about yourself,' I say as I take a sip of the wine. 'You know all about Jamie and me. When was the last time you had someone in your life?'

I'm sure I see his jaw twitch slightly and wonder if it's something he doesn't want to talk about.

'There was someone.' He twirls the stem of his wine glass. 'I thought we were good together, but she wasn't the person I thought she was. She came to Crete to work and ended up staying here. We dated for two years. Everything was going so well. I even thought about asking her to marry me.' He tails off.

'So, what happened?' I ask gently.

'It seemed her secret past caught up with her. We were in the restaurant one day, when her husband from England walked in.'

My hand flies to my mouth.

'Her husband?' I reply in complete shock.

'They were separated, of course. But he tracked her down as he was keen to pursue the divorce.'

'Oh, my goodness, Darius, that must have been awful.'

'I'd certainly had better days.' He attempts a joke. 'It turns out she was definitely not the person I thought she was. It seems she had run up a lot of debt in her husband's name and simply ran away.' He takes a sip of his drink. 'It was hard at the time, but maybe I had a lucky escape. Before that, I was so busy building up the restaurant, I had one or two girlfriends, but nothing really serious for several years. I fell in love with a girl called Aiyana when I was eighteen years old, who broke my heart.' He places his hand on his chest. 'So there, you have my romantic history. Well, most of it,' he says with a glint in his eye. 'But I have never been married.'

'Well, you're not getting my romantic history.' I laugh. 'Not that it's that interesting anyway. Similar to yours really, I suppose.'

'What, an eighteen-year-old girl broke your heart, too?' he says, and it makes me laugh out loud.

'You're such an idiot. I mean, I concentrated on my business too, so I guess we have that in common. I had a couple of boyfriends at college and after one relationship ended, I vowed to stay single. That didn't last though, as a few months later I met Jamie and we were together for four years.'

'That's a long relationship,' he says, regarding me closely. 'But you are okay? You seem to be getting along with things.'

'Yes, I've surprised myself. You never really know how strong you are until you have to be, I suppose.'

Our meals arrive and I devour the delicious lamb *kleftiko*. No wonder people keep flocking here for the food, even in the cooler months. Darius smiles as he eats his beef *stifado* and says it's a good job the restaurant is not in the village, as he wouldn't want the competition.

A little after nine thirty, Darius pays the bill and we are about to head off when I suggest we walk along the beach back to the village.

'If you don't mind,' I say. 'I just love the sound of the sea.'

'Of course. Although there are no more restaurants open

further down the beach, so it may be a little dark,' he reminds me.

'It's fine.'

We walk along the beach, the inky black sea illuminated by a full moon this evening, the sound of the crashing waves soothing my senses. The walk becomes increasingly dark as the lights from the restaurant we dined in fade into the distance. Two old rowing boats are moored up near the water's edge, gently rocking in the waves.

'Have you thought any more about your aunt's restaurant?' I ask as we walk.

'I've thought of little else,' Darius tells me. 'Her restaurant is beautiful and gets busy but I love my life in the village. Actually, maybe you would like to come and look at the restaurant with me sometime, see what you think?'

'Yes, okay. I'd like that.'

Soon we come to a side street, lined with holiday apartments, that leads back to the main street towards the village.

'Well, goodnight then, Darius, thank you for a lovely evening. That restaurant was a real gem,' I tell him as he walks me to my door.

'You are most welcome.' He moves closer and to my surprise, takes my hand and kisses it.

'I will let you know when I am going into Chania. *Kalinichta* Charlotte.'

As he walks off into the moonlight, I raise my hand to my mouth, shocked that I'm imagining how his lips would have tasted against mine. Once again, my feelings are all over the place and I head to bed, more confused than ever.

37

'So, how did it go?'

Katerina and I are sitting in a café on the main road of Agia Marina. It's a perfectly pleasant day, so we decided to walk the half hour it takes to reach the main street. We're in a café with the eye-catching name Fifty Shades of Grill, which has quite a reputation for good food. The owner's son, who served us, tells me he came up with the name after one too many ouzos!

'Oh, it was wonderful.' Katerina has a dreamy look on her face as we dip pitta bread into some delicious dips. 'We went to dinner and then we headed to a bar that had live music. He's so funny, we laughed all evening. And so good looking. I don't think he notices how other women look at him.' She sighs.

'Well, you make a beautiful couple. You're a bit of a head turner yourself, you know.' I can't believe Katerina doesn't see herself as particularly attractive and can't help wondering why.

'Oh stop,' she says, batting away my compliment. The waiter, as if to illustrate my point, turns and casts a lingering glance her way as he heads back to the kitchen.

'I was taken to dinner myself last night,' I reveal, when she has finished telling me all about her date with Ralf.

'Really? You dark horse, who with?'

'Darius. We went to Maria's place on the beach. It was wonderful.'

'I knew he liked you! Well, you also make a perfect couple. He's a lovely man. Do you know he is known in the village as Dreamy Darius?' She giggles.

'Is he really?' I must say I'm not surprised though.

'Yes, he's just so cool. Almost untouchable. At least that's what the women in the village think,' she adds.

'I can see how his appearance might give that impression but I think he's really friendly and down to earth. And just the right side of cheeky,' I say, thinking of his comments and occasional double entendres.

'Well, as I say, I think you would make the perfect couple. I hope it works out for you.'

Our main course arrives and I dine on melt-in-the-mouth pork steak, with a blue cheese sauce that tastes just divine. Katerina says her chicken in an ouzo and tomato sauce is equally delicious.

As our lunch date draws to a close, we head off, deciding to walk home and burn off all the calories. Passing a gift shop, I pop in and buy some herbal tea with lemon and a little metal infuser. Katerina pops into a clothes shop, having spotted a pretty dress displayed in the window at a discount price. Families are strolling along, enjoying the pleasant weather, popping into the shops that are open for a few hours. As we meander, I realise the time is drawing nearer to my phone call with Jamie and I suppress a little feeling of nervousness. Would it be too late to try and work things out if Jamie has had a change of heart? But then, didn't I long for Darius to kiss me when he walked me home last night? As I'm trying to shake off my sense of confusion, we pass a small arcade, where a few teenagers are playing pool and video games and a basketball game stands empty in the corner.

'Shall we shoot a few hoops?' I point to the game.

'Sure, okay.'

I aim the balls through the net, one after the other, impressing some of the teenagers who are watching. As the digital display shows a new high score, I win myself a pink cuddly flamingo.

'That was fun! Who knew you were such a crack shot?' says Katerina as we head off again.

'I was captain of the netball team at school. Seems I haven't lost my goal shooting ability,' I say, strolling along clutching my prize.

Having decided against desserts at the restaurant, we treat ourselves to ice creams and sit on bench in the sunshine to enjoy, just as a family sit beside us, with a young girl who is crying. The mother looks stressed, and when Katerina speaks to her in Greek, she reveals the child has lost the toy rabbit she won on the mini funfair earlier.

I hand my huge pink flamingo to the little girl, whose eyes light up. Her mother thanks me profusely, happy to see the smile return to her little girl's face.

'That was a nice thing you did there,' Katerina comments as we walk on.

'Not really. What would I want with a two-foot flamingo? I'm sure she will appreciate it more than I would.'

We say our goodbyes back at the village. Katerina says she is going to try on her new dress for another date with Ralf that evening. It's been such a wonderful day. I glance at my watch, which shows it's just after four o'clock. Jamie will be calling me in an hour.

I arrive home to see Stelios red-faced and wearing sports gear.

'Stelios, hi! How is the keep-fit going?'

'I would rather be fat,' he grumbles. 'Eleni has even stopped the pastries. It is not good.' He shakes his head.

'Ah, but it is good, well, in the long run at least. You want to live to a ripe old age, don't you?'

'Yes, yes. I know it is good for me. The doctor told me my blood pressure was a little high. Maybe if I work hard now, I can enjoy some of the food at Eleni's party.' He winks.

'That's the spirit. Are you still keeping it a secret from Eleni?'

'Yes. She has no idea.' He speaks like an excited child. 'I think it is the first time I have kept a secret in a long time. Apollo is coming home for the weekend, too.'

I haven't seen Apollo since we talked about him dropping out of medical school.

'Well, it will be nice to catch up with him again,' I tell Stelios as I head inside. 'See you later.'

I busy myself tidying the lounge that doesn't need tidying, plumping up cushions and dusting for the umpteenth time. As I'm putting some plastic bottles into a recycling bin, my phone rings.

'Jamie, hi.'

'Hi, Charlie. How are you?'

It feels so strange hearing his voice that it evokes a mixture of emotions in me.

'I'm doing good, thanks. How are you?'

'A lot better, thanks. Thank God there was no permanent damage, broken ribs and my spleen's gone but I'll live. I'm going back to work next week.'

'I'm so happy you've recovered.'

There's a pause before Jamie is the first to speak.

'Charlie, I... I know it's selfish of me to say so, but I really miss you.'

'What happened to the new girlfriend?'

'It was never anything serious. I never expected her to stick around and nurse me after the accident, we barely knew each other. Mum looked after me when I came out of hospital.'

I imagine Pauline, Jamie's mum, fussing over him and feeding him up with nourishing meals. She was always a great cook.

'You're lucky to have her.'

'I know, she's the best.'

'Jamie,' I say, not even sure what I'm going to say next. 'Why are you calling me? Why now?'

'It's like I told you, I just miss you. I wish I'd been more conscious when you visited me at the hospital.'

'Are you saying you regret moving back to England?' I ask him, getting straight to the point.

'I regret us breaking up.'

'That's not what I asked.'

'Honestly? No, I don't think I do. I never saw Greece as my home like you do. But it doesn't mean I stopped loving you,' he tells me honestly.

'But that's not enough. Listen, Jamie, I understand you might be missing me, but maybe it's because you've had a lot of time to think about things, whilst you've been recovering. I was heartbroken when we broke up, but I've kept busy setting up the shop. I won't lie, being busy has helped me a lot.'

'Maybe you're right. I have had a lot of time to think about stuff whilst I've been healing. Maybe I have a few regrets.'

'But you don't regret moving back to Chester?'

'No. I'm sorry, I told you I was being selfish. I had no right to phone you when you're getting on with your life. I guess I just wanted to hear your voice. I have to ask you though...' He hesitates for a moment. 'Would you ever consider coming home?'

'I am home,' I tell him firmly. 'We both made our choice.'

'I know, I just needed to ask,' he says quietly.

'I'm pleased you're on the mend, Jamie, really I am. And

once you get busy working and living again, you won't think about us so much. I'd like to think we could still be friends though.'

'Really? I'd like that, Charlie, it's better than nothing. I can't imagine never speaking to you again. Maybe when you're back in the UK some time visiting, we could grab a coffee.'

'That would be nice,' I say, realising I actually mean it. We never split acrimoniously; we were just two people following a different path. It will be nice to stay in contact.

'Great. I know we can't turn the clock back, but I'll take being friends,' he says, his tone lighter somehow. 'I was worried you wouldn't want to be.'

'I'd prefer it if there was no animosity, Jamie. I have good memories of our time together. I'll see you in the future, for that coffee.'

'I'll hold you to that. Take care of yourself, Charlie.'

'You too, Jamie, bye.'

Later that evening, I take a glass of wine outside. It is still surprisingly warm and I sit quietly with my thoughts. I replay the conversation with Jamie in my head, feeling as though I have finally put the past behind me. Leaving him in the hospital barely conscious the last time I saw him had been playing on my mind, I realise that now. But he's healing. It was good to know that we can still be friends, or at least civil to each other should our paths cross in the future.

38

'You're in a good mood,' Darius comments as I serve him at the shop the following morning.

'I am,' I say, handing him two cakes in a box, which, if my memory serves right, were the ones he bought last time that I tied with a bow. 'Business is going well; the sun is still shining. Life is good. Would you like a piece of ribbon around the box again?'

'If you have some, yes. My mother was very impressed with that last time.'

His mother? I did wonder who the recipient of the cake was.

'She said your cake was delicious, by the way. Today, I will take her some more.'

'Your mother doesn't live in the village?' I ask as I tie the red ribbon.

'Originally, yes, but she moved closer to Chania after my father died, to be with her sister.'

'The aunt who owned the restaurant?'

'Yes. I think my mother is keen for me to take over the restaurant so I will be closer to her. She lives in the house near the harbour that she shared with my aunt. She has lots of friends but I think she would like her family close by. Kostas has been staying with her this past week.'

'I thought I hadn't seen him around,' I comment.

I go to the other side of the counter and walk him outside while the shop is quiet.

'I think he is a little restless. He always has plenty of work, but he never seems to want to put down roots.'

I recall the conversation we had when Kostas told me he was always putting off the wedding to his fiancée.

'He's always had the wanderlust,' comments Darius.

'Maybe he will settle when he finally finds the one he wants to settle with.'

'Maybe,' Darius says.

'Would your mother ever return to the village?' I ask, before I head into the supermarket for some vanilla extract that we have somehow managed to run out of.

'I am working on that.' He smiles. 'If I decide not to run the restaurant in Chania, I would like her to return. I'm not sure she would be comfortable in my apartment above the restaurant, though. She hates my spiral staircase. Right, I must be going. Thanks for these.' He lifts the box of cakes. 'I will be sure to give you my mother's verdict.'

I find myself imagining the interior of his apartment; the spiral staircase leads me to visualise a cool, stylish place.

He stops halfway to the door of his restaurant and turns around, just as two of his customers approach.

'Are you free for an hour later this evening? I could show you the restaurant in Chania if you like.'

'Sure, why not?'

'Around six o'clock?'

'Perfect. See you later.'

. . .

There's a sudden rush in the next hour, with Katerina constantly replenishing the bread oven and most of the cakes selling out. I whip up some cupcakes with vanilla frosting and a caramel glaze, which prove to be a real hit. By the time we close up for the day, we have sold out of everything.

'Phew. That was a busy day,' I say, as we wash the trays and sweep the floor. 'Not that I'm complaining. I like the sound of the till ringing.'

'Me too. I like to think it means my job is safe,' jokes Katerina.

'I wouldn't have anyone else's big buns.' We both burst out laughing.

I tell Katerina all about heading to Chania to look at the restaurant Darius has been left in his aunt's will. 'Gosh, is he really thinking about leaving the village? It would seem so strange not seeing Darius standing outside his restaurant every day,' she comments.

'I know what you mean, I think he's a little confused himself, so we'll have to wait and see. I'm looking forward to seeing the restaurant though. So how are things with Ralf?' I ask as we head out the door.

'Really good. I told him all about your day at the Botanical Gardens, so he is taking me there on Sunday.'

'I'm glad things are going well.'

'Thank you. It seems your love life is going well too!' She nudges me gently and smiles.

'If you mean Darius and I, we're just good friends,' I tell her, wondering if I'm trying to convince myself. 'Although I do enjoy his company.'

I have a chat with Steph on the phone when I return home. She tells me Matty and Jamie are heading to a football game later and I tell her about my phone call with Jamie.

'I'm glad we can be friends. We've made so many memories together.'

'Me too. Matty said Jamie is relieved about that too,' she tells me. 'So how is village life?'

'Wonderful. Do you know, it's still warm enough for a walk along the beach without a jacket? We actually dined at a beach restaurant recently.'

'Who's we?'

I tell her all about Darius. 'But we're just friends,' I add.

'For now,' Steph teases.

'Oh, I don't know, Steph, I do find him attractive, but I don't want to be rushing into anything,' I confide. 'Besides, it's a small village where everyone knows each other's business. I don't want to be the subject of gossip.'

'So, you're going to stay single because you're worried people might be talking about you?'

'No! It's just that I'm coming to terms with being on my own now. I can feel myself growing braver every day. I'm no longer frightened of the shadows outside the window in the dead of night!'

I remember when we first arrived and I was freaked out by Billy and the sounds of the night owls. Now none of these things bother me. I've even ventured into the olive grove without worrying I might come across a snake. I bake at unsocial hours if I feel like it, or lie on the sofa watching movies in the afternoon. I'm adjusting to a new life and finding out a lot about myself in the process. So far, I have to admit, I quite like what I see.

'What I'm saying,' I continue, 'is that I'm actually enjoying rediscovering myself, I'm not saying I'll be single forever but, for now at least, I'm happy.'

'Makes sense, I suppose. Rebound romances can be a complete disaster. As long as you're happy that's the main thing.'

I ask her about life back home and she tells me a man collapsed in the queue at the bank two days ago and she administered first aid that ultimately saved his life.

'I'd only done my refresher course last month. His wife came into the bank yesterday with a huge bunch of flowers to thank me.'

'Ah, that was nice. Well done you. I bet that was a good feeling.'

'It really was, I've never done anything like that before. It actually made me think about training to be a nurse.'

'Then you should give it some thought! You're young enough to switch careers. It's a big change though, swapping banking for bedpans. Make sure you have a long think about it first,' I advise her sensibly.

'I will. It's just that work at the bank has become a bit too predictable and, well, a bit boring to be honest. I think I'd like the variety nursing brings, every day a bit different. It just feels like such a rewarding career. I couldn't stop thinking about the guy at the bank for days after.'

I think Steph would make a great nurse. She's fun and calm under pressure.

'And maybe you've inspired me a little bit,' she reveals. 'Packing up and doing something completely different and following your dream.'

'Really? Well, thanks for saying so. It feels nice to know that I've inspired someone to do something different. It just takes a bit of courage. And if it doesn't work out, I'm sure you could get a job in a bank again.'

'Yep. I'd turn up like a bad penny,' she jokes.

We wrap up the call and I'm thinking of what a good job Steph would do at cheering up patients, when Darius texts and asks if I will be ready in an hour, so we can set off a little earlier than planned. I check the time – it's just after four o'clock. I tell him that's fine before I head upstairs for a shower.

39

The Olympia Bar and Grill looks resplendent bathed in late afternoon sunlight, shafts of light reflecting from the pale walls. Diners are sitting outside at tables that are covered in white linen tablecloths, with fresh flowers in clear vases set in the middle of the tables. Good-looking couples, wearing sunglasses and enjoying the late afternoon sun, are sharing bottles of wine and engaging in conversation.

'Wow, this is nice. It looks very upmarket,' I comment.

'Wait until you see inside.'

Darius leads the way and we enter a large indoor dining room, with white marble floors, wooden tables and gold-coloured chandeliers. Smartly dressed waiters serve delicious-looking food. It's opulent without feeling stuffy and the sound of people's chatter and laughter can be heard ringing around the restaurant.

'Darius! *Kalispera.*'

A man who looks to be in his late forties approaches us and shakes Darius by the hand. Darius introduces him as the head chef. He seems to have been called into the dining room to receive compliments from a large party, who are still applauding him.

'I see you are still keeping the customers happy. My aunt would be very proud.'

'I am so sorry for your loss. Your aunt was such a wonderful woman. Your mother calls in regularly to make sure standards are not slipping.'

'I can imagine.' Darius laughs.

'In fact,' he says, glancing at his watch, 'she should be here shortly; I have your table ready.'

He summons a waiter to show us to a table, as I process the shock fact that Darius's mother will be joining us.

'I didn't realise your mother would be coming too,' I say, suddenly and inexplicably feeling a little nervous.

'Oh, I'm sorry, I thought it made more sense to dine together. I would have had to call at her house otherwise, which would have felt a little formal. Do you mind?' he asks, pouring us both some iced water from a jug.

'No, of course not.' I smile brightly.

Five minutes later, an impossibly glamorous woman, with dark hair piled up on her head and wearing an expensive-looking red dress, glides across the floor towards us. She is escorted by an equally attractive gentleman of a similar age, wearing white slacks and shirt, with a navy blazer over the top.

'Darius, my darling.' She kisses him on both cheeks before introducing her gentleman friend, Hector. Darius then introduces me to his mother, Helen.

'Ah yes! The exquisite baker.' She takes my hands in hers and kisses me on both cheeks. I inhale her beautiful perfume. 'Your cakes are so lovely, although I probably shouldn't indulge quite so much.' She laughs. Despite being intimidatingly glamorous, she has a friendly manner that immediately puts me at ease.

She is tall and elegant, and not at all how I imagined somehow. I visualised a homely Greek lady who looked forward to Darius visiting, pouring tea and eating cake.

When Hector nips to the bathroom, Darius turns to his mother.

'You never told me you were bringing a new boyfriend along.'

'Touché.' She raises an eyebrow and I blush.

'We are simply friends,' he tells his mother and I feel an irrational sense of disappointment.

'As are Hector and I.' She smiles. 'Actually, we are heading to the theatre after dinner to watch a musical. You are most welcome to join us. Hector only booked the tickets earlier today and there were still plenty of seats available.'

'Thank you, I do love the theatre, but I'm afraid I'm a little underdressed,' I say politely.

I wish Darius had told me that we were having dinner in such a smart restaurant. My plain cotton dress seems more suitable for a day's sightseeing.

'Me too,' says Darius, who is wearing a short-sleeved shirt and shorts. 'But another time, Mother, I promise.'

'Well, alright.' She seems satisfied.

We dine on the most delicious seafood bathed in a creamy garlic sauce. There are Parmentier potatoes, courgettes, and colourful peppers. A stunning ice-cream dish served in a sponge case and drizzled in chocolate is presented for dessert. The menu offers moussaka and other traditional foods along with some more fine-dining dishes. There's something for everyone, so it's no surprise the place is so popular.

'That was wonderful, as usual.' Helen wipes her mouth with a napkin. 'After coffee, we really ought to be leaving.' She glances at her watch.

Fifteen minutes later she and Hector stand to leave.

'It was so lovely to meet you, Charlotte. I hope you can talk some sense into my son and persuade him to run this restaurant.' She winks as she picks up a gold lamé clutch bag from the table. Darius rolls his eyes and smiles.

'I have told you, Mother, I will give it some thought.'

Helen kisses us both goodbye and Hector grips us each with a firm handshake.

'Well, that was a surprise,' I say, as Darius and I stroll along the pier later that evening. The navy sky is becoming dotted with sparkly white stars. 'I thought I was simply coming to give the restaurant the once over.'

'Sorry about that. My mother mentioned she would be dining there. I couldn't bring myself to tell you, in case you thought I was purposefully taking you along to meet my mother.'

'Oh, don't worry about it. She's really lovely, I'm glad I met her. She seems keen for you to take over the management of the restaurant.'

'She does. But she enjoys living in Chania, so she is being entirely selfish,' he says, but with a smile playing around his lips. 'But if Kostas wants to sell the restaurant, I may have no choice in the matter. It would be a wrench leaving the village anyway. Especially now.'

'Why now?'

We're standing beneath an old-fashioned street lamp on a cobbled path, the soft light illuminating Darius's handsome features.

'Because I've become rather partial to your delicious cakes.'

I push him gently on the arm and he turns to face me.

'And now, I may just be doing something that ruins our friendship, but I can't help myself.'

Without warning he takes me gently by the hand, and pulls me towards him. A part of me doesn't want this to happen, yet standing here, with the twinkling lights from the restaurants reflecting on the dark water behind us, I feel almost powerless to resist. I don't want this, I tell myself. I don't want to get involved, but my body doesn't seem to be paying any attention. Our lips are about to meet when a voice calls out.

'Watch out! Mia, slow down!'

Suddenly, a child on a bike brushes against me, pushing me hard into Darius, as a man gives chase. The moment is broken.

As we head back to the car, I feel conflicted once more, as I wonder how a kiss on the lips would have felt.

40

In the days that follow, I immerse myself in work, experimenting with new cake flavours, always being unavailable when Darius asks me out. Yesterday, he jokingly asked me if I was avoiding him, and I laughed it off, telling him I'm simply busy, which is only partly true. The real truth is, I want to give myself some space from him to try and figure out my feelings.

It's Eleni's party in two weeks, so I am also genuinely busy thinking up some new ideas for the catering, as well as making some new cushion covers and curtains in autumn shades for the lounge, having dragged out my old sewing machine that I haven't used in years. I'm also promoting the website a little more, in the hope of securing some bookings for the annexe next year. And, to be honest, it's all a welcome distraction. I'm still not sure I want the complication of a new love in my life, no matter how attractive Darius is. Besides, he still hasn't decided whether or not he will take over his aunt's restaurant, and taking the helm at such a huge restaurant, I'm sure I'd hardly ever see him.

I spoke to Milly last night, and she said I was probably doing the right thing by not rushing into something new, although Steph told me I should 'Get back on the horse and have a little fun,' which made me laugh.

I've found myself on more than one occasion wondering what might have happened, had the child on the bike not ruined the moment between us. Would I have gone back to Darius's flat and then woken, filled with regret the next morning? There's no doubt I can feel the heat between us when we stand so close. I don't know, perhaps Steph is right after all.

I hear a noise in the garden and look up. 'Good morning, Leo, how are you doing?'

'I'm okay. My back hurts a little today, if I tell you the truth, but it will disappear when I work. It just takes me a little longer to get started in the mornings these days.' He smiles.

'If you're sure it isn't too much for you?' I tell him.

'Not at all! I love to be in the garden,' he reassures me. 'My brother only has a small outside space. The garden is the thing I miss about this house.'

Over the last few days, the pool has been emptied and covered and my basil plant, which sits in a huge pot, has been brought indoors. The pale-yellow leaves from the trees are still gently falling, and Leo continues to rake them into a mound before disposing of them. Sometimes when he has finished his work, he will have coffee with Stelios or head to a game of dominoes at the village bar with him, where they will happily spend a couple of hours playing and putting the world to rights.

It's Sunday today, so I have the rest of the day stretching ahead. I'm thinking about what to do when Katerina calls.

'Hi, Charlotte, are you free today? I wondered if you fancied taking a walk somewhere?'

'Hi, Kat, yes, actually, I am. I just have a few things to finish up here, I'll be ready in an hour?'

'Great I'll walk down later. Bye.'

Just over an hour later, she arrives wearing cut-off jeans, a white T-shirt and a light pink fleece. I feel blessed that we seem to be experiencing a mild autumn and I dress similarly, but with a long-sleeved top instead of a fleece.

'Do you want to walk from here, or do you fancy going to Lake Agia?' I ask, which is around a twenty-minute drive away. 'I haven't been there yet, but Kostas told me it was pretty.'

'That sounds like a lovely idea,' agrees Kat.

'I thought you might be seeing Ralf today,' I say, as we climb into the car and head off.

'I've seen him three times this week but today I felt like spending some time alone, well, with a friend.'

'Is everything okay?'

'It's fine, but I think maybe things are moving a little too fast for me.'

'Really? And to think you weren't even sure if he was interested in you,' I say.

'I know. Don't get me wrong, I think he's wonderful, but he always seems to be pointing out houses for sale and talking about mortgages. Maybe it's because he works in a bank.' She laughs. 'I just get the feeling he is ready to settle down. He's even talked about having children, saying how he loved being part of a large family.'

'And you don't want those things?'

'I do eventually, just not yet,' she explains. 'I want to spend a few years travelling and having some fun first. I've never even been to Athens, which I long to visit one day!'

'Have you told him how you feel?' I ask, thinking of how vital communication is and how I wish Jamie had been more open with me about his feelings when we moved here. I think Katerina and Ralf are made for each other and would hate any misunderstandings to ruin things between them.

'Not really. I don't want to spoil what we have, but I don't want to rush into things either, if you see what I mean?'

'As it happens, I do.' I tell Kat all about my near kiss with Darius and the circles that are going around in my head about it. 'So, you see, I know exactly what you mean. Although Darius isn't talking about houses and children!'

'What are we like?' Kat sighs. 'Two gorgeous men wanting our attention and yet we hesitate.'

'I guess it's just the timing for me,' I tell her. 'I'm only a few months out of a long relationship. I don't want to just rush into another one.'

'Well, I agree with my mother, who says if things are meant to be, then they will be. Maybe we both just need to relax.'

'That sounds like sensible advice. Talking about travelling more, though, you ought to start by booking a trip to Athens! Take Ralf with you. The flights aren't too expensive from Chania. I'm sure I could manage without you for a few days.' Kat has taught me how to make the bread buns, so I'm sure I can manage in the shop on my own for a day or two.

'Really?' Kat swings her head around with a look of surprise on her face.

'Of course. You'll just have to ask Ralf, although I don't think he will take much persuading.'

Kat claps her hands together. 'Wonderful, I'll ask him.'

After parking the car, we head towards the blue-green lake, which has a footpath surrounding it. Crossing a blue-painted wooden bridge, we arrive in a forest glade, where families are enjoying picnics at wooden benches. Children are running about, two small boys kicking a football as the sun filters through the leaves of the towering trees. It's a place for sublime relaxation and it's lovely to see families enjoying their Sundays together.

An hour later, having taken a circular walk around the lake, we head to the pretty café that has floor-length glass windows, giving a wonderful view of the lake. Pots of tall ferns are dotted about the interior on the light wooden flooring. There are stone fountains of water and Buddha statues giving the place a feeling of calm and serenity. Inside, the menu has organic snacks and healthy food platters. We both choose a tempting chicken and hummus wrap and a rocket and beetroot salad with a frothy cappuccino.

'What a lovely place for a stroll,' I tell Kat as we sip our coffees. 'Just what I needed today, thanks for the suggestion.'

'It's what I needed too. I'm glad you came to the village and we became friends.'

'Me too.'

Kat's friends had been keen to marry early and have children, so she didn't often have the time for single girlie pursuits at weekends.

'It's Eleni's party in two weeks. Do you think she will like the surprise?' asks Kat, once we've paid the bill and are heading towards the car park.

'I hope so. Stelios has gone to a lot of trouble to keep it secret. He tells me Apollo has been working on a painting of his mother, too. He's a very talented artist apparently.'

'I'm glad he's doing what he loves,' Kat says. 'I just hope Stelios isn't too disappointed that he isn't going to become a doctor. It's all Stelios has spoken about in the village for years.'

'I think he's accepted it now. He realises Apollo gets his artistic talent from him. Stelios had done the most marvellous sculpture of Eleni himself, but I'm not sure it will ever be on general display.'

I tell her all about it and she laughs.

'Well, I think that is really romantic. I would love it if a man did something so wonderful as to sculpt my image!'

'This has been such a lovely afternoon.' Kat kisses me on both cheeks when we arrive back at the village. 'Thank you, Charlotte. I'm seeing Ralf this evening. I can't wait to ask him about a weekend in Athens! Enjoy the rest of your evening.'

'I loved today too. See you bright and early in the morning.'

'Don't remind me! I'm usually fine with the early mornings, but Mondays? Ugh.' She laughs before heading off.

That evening, I have a long chat with Milly, who is still enjoying spending time with Simon, the guy she met in the library. Today they took both boys on a trip to the museum to see a display of dinosaurs and they've been to the planetarium too.

'We all get along so well, I'm thrilled,' she tells me.

Later, I do a little baking and watch a film about a woman who meets the most wonderful man, but she keeps him at arm's length because she's been hurt, and I smile at how art is imitating my life at the moment.

41

It's a busy Monday morning and it isn't until twelve thirty that the rush has eased and I'm able to nip home to collect my phone that I forgot and left charging there.

Passing The Fig Tree, I notice Darius stepping into his Audi, joined by a stunning brunette with long, straight hair, wearing a blue floral dress. I watch from a distance as they drive off, a knot of something in my stomach. Suddenly I'm annoyed with myself. What if he is taking someone out? We're not in a relationship, and I've been the one gently pushing him away these past couple of weeks. But I can't help feeling that I really shouldn't allow myself to develop feelings for someone who is clearly a playboy.

I locate my phone and pop it into my bag before walking back to the bakery, suddenly feeling a little flat.

Kat is giddy with excitement when I arrive, telling me that Ralf has just called into the shop to let her know that he has booked a break to Athens for two weeks' time.

'We're staying in a hotel near a busy square right in the heart of the city,' she tells me excitedly. 'We're going to take the bus tour and see the Olympic Stadium and the Acropolis,' she babbles happily. 'Apollo told him it's the best way to see the city.'

'That sounds wonderful. I'm really thrilled for you.' I muster a smile.

'Is everything okay?' Kat asks a little later, as we tidy away before closing up.

'What? Yeah, I think so. I'm just a little tired. I probably stayed up far later than I should have done last night watching a movie.'

I don't want to tell her about Darius, as it was only yesterday that I was telling her that I don't want to rush into things. 'I'll be fine after an early night,' I tell her, smiling once more.

'Okay and thanks again for allowing me the time to go away, it's something I never really got to do when I was looking after the boys. Oh and I actually had a long talk with Ralf last night, and he laughed and said he wasn't ready for babies and houses yet either. He said he can't help commenting on houses because he's a mortgage advisor, which was what I thought. He even said he would wait forever for me, which was really sweet of him.'

'I'm really happy for you, Kat.'

I bump into Eleni outside the supermarket when I finish work, and she tells me she is going to the cinema later to watch a screening of *Chicago* and will be having some food beforehand with friends.

'You are most welcome to join us,' she offers and I find myself accepting.

'Wonderful. See you later. We will leave at six and eat before the show starts at eight.'

My days are so busy with the shop, and of course I have Kat, but I think it's time I made an effort to make some more friends. I've learned that there are walking groups that leave from the village bar and even a cycling club that meet near the beach every Sunday. I've met some of Eleni's friends, who vary in age, so at least the cinema trip is a start in widening my circle a little.

Just after ten o'clock, we arrive home after a delightful evening. The women were all lovely. One or two I had already met at Eleni's house and they brought their daughters along, all around my age, which was wonderful. As we left, they whispered they would see me at Eleni's party, which is still a closely guarded secret.

A short while later, settling down in bed, I think of how blessed I am. I chose to have my life here in Crete, as I have always adored Greece. But I've also come to realise that to be part of a community you have to embrace it wholeheartedly and accept invitations. I think of Milly's words, telling me I should find a work-life balance, or what is the point of relocating here? I'm happily carving out the life I really want for myself and it feels amazing.

42

It's the afternoon of Eleni's party and Stelios is dashing around like a headless chicken.

'Now, you are sure we have everything ready?' He's pacing my kitchen, a worried look on his face.

'Relax, everything is under control here. Have you spoken to Darius about the hot food? And did you say you have organised some entertainment?' I ask.

I realise I haven't spoken to Darius properly for at least a few days, busying myself with other tasks when I finish work at the bakery.

'Apollo will be arriving in around one hour, which will be a surprise to his mother. Some of Apollo's friends are in a band and they are going to play. The lead singer has the most wonderful voice. Did I ever tell you that I could have been a singer?'

He launches into one of his stories about how he was almost signed up by a record producer when he was in his teens, singing in a bar.

'You're lucky to be a man of many talents,' I say. He nods in agreement, which makes me smile.

'There is just one thing I worry about,' he confides. 'Eleni does not like to go to the bar much these days. Also, she said she does not want a fuss for her birthday. What if she refuses to go out this evening?'

Eleni's birthday is actually tomorrow, but Stelios has chosen Saturday evening for the celebration as tomorrow is a day of rest for many people.

'I'm sure you are worrying over nothing,' I try to reassure him, although in truth I can't really be certain. Eleni confided to me at the cinema evening how she preferred restaurants and shows to the local bar, as it's mostly just full of men loudly playing card games and dominoes.

'I think if you tell her there will be live entertainment, it might just swing it,' I tell him. 'You know how much she likes music.'

'Wonderful idea! I am so looking forward to eating some delicious food, it *is* a party after all and I have lost a little weight.' He pats his stomach, which actually does look a little more streamlined.

'I thought you were looking svelte. All those beach walks have paid off.'

'And not so many of your cakes. I am sorry, my diet may have been bad for business.' He roars with laughter.

A short while later, I'm about to drive to a nearby market for some fresh salad for finishing touches, when my phone rings. I'm surprised to hear the voice of Darius at the other end.

'Hi, Darius.'

'Hello, Charlotte, I was wondering, are you free today?'

'I'm about to head out to a food market,' I tell him. 'I need a few finishing touches for the party food.'

'In that case, if you do not mind, may I join you?'

I'm surprised by his request but agree to it and five minutes later he is walking towards me looking attractive in jeans and a long-sleeved black shirt. As he draws closer, I'm surprised to see that he is sporting the faint outline of a black eye.

'What happened to you?' I ask.

'I will tell you on the drive.'

In the car, Darius tells me he went to the assistance of one of the waitresses at the restaurant, whose ex-boyfriend was refusing to let her collect some things from his apartment after a break-up.

'Including a ring that she'd been given by her grandmother. He sounded like a bad lot. She was worried he might sell it. She had no one else to ask. Her father disowned her after she started the relationship, thinking the guy was bad news. It turns out he was right.'

'So, I take it he put up a fight then? The cheeky sod.'

'He did. He only opened the door after I threatened him with the police. Once inside, he became aggressive to Phoebe and managed to land a sneaky punch on me when I stood between them. I am not a believer in violence, but I forcibly restrained him until the police arrived.'

'Gosh, that's a brave thing to do! It must have been awful.'

'I must admit I have had better days. The good thing is, Phoebe got all her belongings back, including the ring.'

So, Phoebe was the young woman with the long dark hair who had climbed into the car with Darius. I think how kind it was of him to offer his support when Phoebe had no one else to turn to. Maybe he's just been helping her out all along and I've jumped to the wrong conclusions about his playboy ways.

Ten minutes later, we park up before walking into the bustling market square, flanked by old buildings, and apartments with Juliet balconies. There's a white church with a blue wooden door on one side of the market, a flower stall directly outside, selling colourful blooms of every description.

I buy some juicy tomatoes and a bag of fresh lemons, as my home-grown ones are in short supply now. I buy bunches of fresh herbs and rocket to adorn platters of sandwiches. Moving on, I buy some fresh, delicious salamis and a tasty-looking cooked pork, flavoured with cinnamon and smoked paprika. Darius also buys some fresh herbs and cloves for the finishing touches of his huge chicken casserole for this evening's party.

The square is buzzing with traders selling jars of honey, ouzo and raki. There are stands offering crusty breads dotted with olives and sun-dried tomatoes, alongside stalls selling tempting home-made pies of meats, spinach and feta. It's a mild November day and a watery sun is breaking through the clouds as we walk from stall to stall. On the opposite side of the food market are traders selling clothes and bags and I spot a beautiful navy leather handbag that has a pretty gold chain.

'You like your handbags, don't you?' remarks Darius, as I find myself unable to resist and hand over the money.

'You've noticed.' I smile.

'I notice everything about you.' He locks eyes with me and I once again feel the colour rise in my cheeks. 'I think maybe you have a different colour for every day of the week.'

'And more, probably! Although I do have my favourites.'

Laden down with shopping, we go to a café for a drink before heading off home.

'I feel a bit guilty sitting here.' I glance at my watch. 'I feel as though I have a lot to do.'

'You always seem to be in a hurry. Especially these last few weeks.' He sips his coffee. 'You should enjoy life, slow down a little.'

I think of how I've barely spoken to him lately, dashing off to do things that could probably have waited, in an attempt to erase him from my thoughts.

'Maybe you're right. Things are so laid-back here. Perhaps it just takes a little time to get used to the pace.'

And it's true, I probably don't need to dash off. The cakes, bread rolls and pies are all prepared. Most of them already dropped at the bakery, which is close to the bar. I just have to prepare some sandwiches and coleslaw later, and it's barely noon right now.

Sitting here, sipping a cappuccino as the sun finally breaks through, fills me with a sense of contentment.

'You have spent a whole summer here now,' says Darius as he sips his coffee. 'Any regrets?'

'Honestly? No. I'm enjoying life here. And I've made lots of new friends.'

I tell him all about my night at the cinema, as well as my good friendship with Katerina.

'I think I made the right decision in coming here. I can't imagine living anywhere else now.'

'Me neither,' reveals Darius. 'I've decided to stay in the village.'

'Really?' I say in surprise.

'Yes. Before my aunt passed away, the manager at the restaurant was not so good, so she hoped I might take over. But Nico, the man in charge now, is terrific. Business is really good. My mother likes him too.' He smiles. 'I don't think the restaurant needs my presence.'

'Was your mother disappointed?'

'I don't think so. She's been seeing rather a lot of her new friend Hector.' He raises an eyebrow.

We finish our drinks and drive back to the village, chatting about the party this evening.

'Stelios is worried Eleni won't want to go out tonight. He was in a bit of a panic this morning,' I tell Darius.

'I'm sure it will be alright. Stelios can be very persuasive.'

'I'm sure you're right.'

'Do you need help with anything?' Darius offers when he steps out of the car outside the restaurant.

'No, thanks, I think everything is under control. I'll see you later.'

As I walk up the path to my house, Billy is standing near the kitchen door.

'There you are! Where have you been lately?'

Billy nods and brays.

'Or maybe you know there's a party tonight? Sorry but most of the food is at the bakery. Besides, I'm not quite sure I've forgiven you for eating my favourite sunhat.'

Billy hangs his head as if in shame and I wonder whether he actually understands me.

'It's a pretty carefree life you have, isn't it? Wandering about wherever you feel like and maybe being given some treats. Shall I see if I have anything in the fridge?'

Billy nods his head, and when I open the door, he tries to follow me inside.

'Sorry, but don't overstep the mark. We can be friends as long as you know your boundaries,' I tell him firmly, wondering if I have finally lost the plot.

Inside, I find some slightly stale bread and green salad in the fridge and offer it to Billy. I sit outside for half an hour, enjoying some unexpected sunshine with Billy keeping me company, before he's finally had enough and trots off.

'See you later then. Don't be getting on anyone's goat.'

43

The village bar looks unrecognisable, Eleni's friends having worked hard with balloons and flower displays, covering the dark tables with white tablecloths.

The buffet is laid out on a long table next to the bar itself. A stage has been erected in the outdoor area for the band to perform on later, and lights have been threaded through the trees. I'm putting the finishing touches to things, when Darius arrives with a huge cauldron of casserole that he takes into the small kitchen at the rear of the building.

'Well, this all looks wonderful.' He eyes the food already set out on the long table, which does look rather lovely, if I say so myself. There are savoury pies, quiches, salads, and sandwiches, as well as crusty rolls stuffed with a variety of tasty fillings. Trays of strawberry tarts and vanilla slices sit either side of a huge birthday cake in the centre of the table, decorated with pink and white roses.

'I'll see you later. I'm heading off to shower and change,' Darius says, checking his watch.

Darius told me that he is closing the restaurant for the evening, as business is winding down for the winter.

Although I imagine half the village will be here tonight anyway.

'Me too. See you shortly.'

Just after six thirty, I message Stelios and ask if everything is going to plan and breathe a sigh of relief when he sends me a thumbs up and a smiling face emoji.

It takes me a long time to decide what I should wear: half a dozen outfits are flung on the bed as I think them unsuitable. The last time I went to a party was the leaving BBQ we had back in Milly's garden. I wore a floral dress as the weather was warm at the time and, rooting through my wardrobe, I realise that most of my clothes consist of summer dresses or winter woollies and not much in between. I'm about to give up and wear some smart jeans with one of my favourite pink tops, when I come across a long black dress with a V-neck. A bargain I sourced in a Ghost sale back home. I slip it on and it looks perfect, especially when I add a pretty silver necklace. I scrunch some mousse through my newly washed hair, which is behaving itself this evening for a change, and it falls into soft curls. A spritz of scent, and I'm ready to go.

I'm almost at the front gate, when I spot Eleni leaving the house. She is followed by Apollo, who is dressed in jeans and a fashionable black shirt with a colourful pattern, and Stelios, who is in a grey suit with a loud yellow shirt underneath.

'Charlotte,' she calls me over. 'Wow, you look beautiful this evening, are you going somewhere special?'

Eleni looks stunning in a jade-green dress and her hair piled up.

'Er, yes, somewhere very special.' I glance at Stelios, who shrugs.

'I am going for a wonderful meal for my birthday with my husband and brilliant son, who has surprised me by coming home! But first we are having a little drink at the village bar. Do you have time to join us?' she asks.

I hate deceiving Eleni in this way, but it is a surprise party after all.

'Yes, that would be lovely, thanks.'

My stomach is churning as we head towards the bar, worrying she will turn on her heels and flee when she sees all the guests inside.

'You are all looking very smart too,' I say as we walk and chat about our respective days.

Apollo is on his phone, furiously texting someone, as Eleni and I chat amongst ourselves. As we approach the bar, Eleni is surprised that it appears to be plunged into darkness, the daylight already faded in the now almost-winter months. A glance at the outside area visible through a gate shows the pretty lights twisted through the trees.

'Maybe people are outside,' I suggest. 'It is a mild evening after all.'

Eleni has a puzzled look on her face until Stelios pushes the door open and the lights come on. A chorus of people startle her as they shout, 'Surprise!'

She stands open-mouthed for a second, taking in the scene in front of her. The bar looks so pretty and her family and friends are clapping their hands and smiling. All of a sudden, she bursts into tears.

'Oh no, have I made a mistake?' Stelios cuddles his wife, but she bats him away as her face, thankfully, breaks into a smile.

'No. Stelios, it's wonderful.' She looks at her husband lovingly and he visibly breathes a sigh of relief.

Outside, the sound of the band strikes up as people step forward to wish Eleni a happy birthday and place gifts on a table. Stelios proposes a toast to Eleni, saying she grows more beautiful with every year that passes, which draws loving sighs from the crowd.

People are taking seats, and Pepe and two bartenders serve them drinks at their tables. I'm removing covers from the buffet dishes when Darius walks in and I catch my breath. He's wearing a light blue suit, with an open-necked white shirt underneath. His hair looks recently styled and as he strides forward, he catches the eye of almost every woman in the room.

'Charlotte.' I look up at him and he kisses me on both cheeks. 'You look sensational,' he whispers.

'So do you,' I say, returning the compliment.

People chat and eat from the buffet and, later on, two young waiters serve the delicious casserole made by Darius in bowls at the table with pitta bread and pickled cabbage. Everyone is having the most wonderful evening, and a little after nine thirty, the band strikes up outside. Katerina arrives with Ralf, both of them looking gorgeous, and they join us for drinks.

The outside area looks absolutely beautiful and the band sing some songs in Greek that I don't understand, but Stelios was right about the lead singer having a wonderful voice. Apollo has kindly asked his friends to sing a couple of songs in English, and when a Michael Bublé song filters through the air, Darius asks me to dance.

'May I?' He leads me by the hand and I follow, dancing slowly and inhaling the smell of his aftershave. Ralf and Katerina sway to the music beside us and, when I catch her gaze, she winks at me.

I feel Darius's fingers gently running up and down my spine, sending thrills through my body as we move to the melody. I'm enjoying every second when suddenly the song finishes and Stelios grabs the microphone and tells everyone that it's time to light some candles on the cake.

'But not all of them. We don't want a fire in the bar,' he jokes.

It's a wonderful party; people have danced the night away and it seems as though Apollo's friends may have some more bookings for their band in the near future. As the evening draws to a close, a group of us are sitting inside sipping champagne and chatting.

'I don't know how you kept this a secret.' Eleni leans into Stelios and he wraps his arms around her. 'I've had the most wonderful time.'

'It was difficult. I find it hard to keep anything from you.' He kisses the top of her head, moving aside the strands of colourful streamers threaded through her hair.

'And Charlie and Darius, I cannot thank you enough for the wonderful food.'

'It was our pleasure,' says Darius, and Eleni, slightly tipsily, tells him that our names sound great together.

Stelios tells Eleni he thought she would be mad at him for organising the party as she told him she didn't want a fuss.

'Women don't always mean what they say,' she tells him and once more he looks puzzled.

'Would you like to get some fresh air?' Darius asks me, and Stelios and Eleni look at each other knowingly.

'Sure, why not?'

We walk outside into the pretty yard, the lights still shining in the trees, to find there's a full moon shining in the navy sky.

'I am hoping,' says Darius, as he circles his arms around my waist and draws me in to him, 'that there will be no more interruptions this time. I have waited so long to do this.'

Finally, his lips meet mine and fireworks seem to explode all around as he draws me closer.

We finally pull apart and he takes a breath. 'Well, that was definitely worth waiting for.'

'Darius,' I say, my head spinning with joy. 'There's no denying the attraction between us, but you may need to give me a little time. I wasn't planning on falling in love again.'

'That's okay. How does the song go? "You Can't Hurry Love"?' he says, before moving in for another kiss.

I look into his eyes. 'You certainly can't. Not if it is to last.'

'I hope it will. In the meantime, we can spend time just enjoying ourselves.' He draws me close to him and kisses me once more.

'That's fine with me,' I breathe, and despite my caution, at this very moment, I am bursting with happiness. As he gazes into my eyes, those fireworks seem to be going off again.

'There's a line in another song that reminds me that we have all the time in the world,' says Darius, as he holds me close.

'I can't argue with that.' I look into his dark eyes. 'Let's just see what happens in Greece...'

A LETTER FROM SUE ROBERTS

Dear reader,

I want to say a huge thank you for choosing to read *What Happens in Greece*. If you did enjoy it, and want to keep up to date with all my latest releases, just sign up at the following link. Your email address will never be shared and you can unsubscribe at any time.

www.bookouture.com/sue-roberts

I do enjoy it when readers message me to tell me how they've enjoyed reading my books from a sunny beach, or equally how it brightens up a miserable day, when they are stuck indoors! Wherever you read, I am happy you chose one of my books to escape from everyday life.

I hope you loved *What Happens in Greece* and, if you did, I would be very grateful if you could write a review. I'd love to hear what you think, and it makes such a difference helping new readers to discover one of my books for the first time.

I love hearing from my readers – you can get in touch on my Facebook page, through Twitter, Goodreads or my website.

Huge thanks,

Sue Roberts

KEEP IN TOUCH WITH SUE

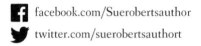

facebook.com/Suerobertsauthor

twitter.com/suerobertsauthort